Dr. Norman Jones is founder and head of the consulting firm Communications Unlimited, which promotes interpersonal communication skills. He has made presentations for numerous companies and organizations, such as Allstate, Blue-Cross–Blue-Shield and the University of Wisconsin football staff. Dr. Jones is also past President of the Northwest Suburban Chapter of the Illinois Guidance and Personnel Association.

*The obscure we see eventually,
the completely apparent takes longer.*
EDWARD R. MURROW

Keep in Touch

How to Communicate Better by Responding to the Feeling Instead of the Event

Norman Jones

A SPECTRUM BOOK

Prentice-Hall, Inc., Englewood Cliffs, New Jersey 07632

Library of Congress Cataloging in Publication Data

Jones, Norman,
  Keep in touch.

  (A Spectrum Book)
  Includes bibliographies and index.
1. Interpersonal communication. 2. Interpersonal
relations. I. Title.
BF637.C45J68   158'.2   81-10733
                                  AACR2

ISBN 0-13-514778-6

ISBN 0-13-514760-3 [PBK.]

A Spectrum Book

Printed in the United States of America

10 9 8 7 6 5 4 3 2 1

This Spectrum Book can be made available to
businesses and organizations at a special discount
when ordered in large quantities. For more information
contact: Prentice-Hall, Inc., General Book Marketing,
Special Sales Division, Englewood Cliffs, N.J. 07632.

Prentice-Hall International, Inc., *London*
Prentice-Hall of Australia Pty., Limited, *Sydney*
Prentice-Hall of Canada, Ltd., *Toronto*
Prentice-Hall of India Private, Limited, *New Delhi*
Prentice-Hall of Japan, Inc., *Tokyo*
Prentice-Hall of Southeast Asia Pte., Ltd., *Singapore*
Whitehall Books, Limited, *Wellington, New Zealand*

"*Keep in Touch* is brilliantly done. Norm Jones writes with warmth and sensitivity constantly helping the reader to grow without feeling guilty about his or her previous mistakes. I highly recommend this book for anyone who works or lives with people—and who doesn't? Glances at the treasures that Jones gives to the reader will undoubtedly change relationships in positive ways whether the relationships involve parenting, teaching, counseling, selling, or supervising. This one is a winner!"

DR. LEWIS E. LOSONCY
(Author of *Turning People On,*
You Can Do It, and
The Encouragement Book)

"Frankly, I have read several books on communicating with people and none hit the bull's-eye like this one. The ideas and methods can be applied by any person in whatever field he or she is involved."

DAVE McCLAIN
Head Football Coach
University of Wisconsin—Madison

"The basic relationship skills presented in *Keep in Touch* are the foundation upon which counselors and therapists in training will build their intervention techniques. They are the *sine qua non* of effective therapeutic work in any setting, be it individual, group, or relationship counseling. Because of his writing style, Jones' work is appropriate for professionals and lay people alike."

DR. WILLIAM M. WALSH
Counselor Education Department
Northeastern Illinois University
(Author of *A Primer
in Family Therapy*)

Contents

Foreword

Keep in Touch is concerned with helping readers improve their skills in human relationships. It recognizes that we all have life-long patterns of ineffective interpersonal responses. These responses are the result of our transactions with our parents, siblings, peers, and eventually our expanded social milieu. In the process of growing up, we developed a set of beliefs or mistaken assumptions that interfere with effective interpersonal relations.

Jones has built upon the interpersonal communication concepts originally set forth by Alfred Adler and Harry Stack Sullivan, and later researched in detail by Robert Carkhuff, George Gazda, and Allen Ivey. However, the book is not a technical manual but is directed at the person who wants to make a change in his or her interpersonal relationships. The book, then, serves well all those who are involved with people such as parents, teachers, supervisors, employees, and so on.

One of the major messages is to respond to feelings rather than to the event. That is, to hear what is going on in the speaker, and by comprehending feelings, intentions, beliefs, and attitudes, to develop a response that indicates understanding and empathy.

As Virginia Satir has indicated, communication is effective when our words and our feelings coincide. We are congruent when we state what we feel and at the same time give other persons room to share their meanings with us.

Jones gives some very basic rules to help the reader respond differently:

1. Understand the feeling, not the event. Respond to the theme and the energy that are involved in the methods, not the surface communication.
2. In responding, use a feeling word. This is easier said than done, but it suggests that we expand our vocabulary of feeling words and that we care enough to become involved with the other person on the basis of his or her feelings.
3. Eliminate questions. Questions usually put the other person on the defensive and do not lead to open communication.
4. Eliminate logic and assumptions. These are forms of interpretation that are not appropriate.
5. Don't offer solutions or give advice. The evidence is that the other person will act more often on the solutions he creates than on the advice you give.
6. Allow the other person to do the talking. Just simple listening is an effective way of establishing contact.
7. Eliminate evaluations, opinions, and judgments. Help the other person become self-evaluative.

The book closes with perhaps the most valuable part, the practical applications of how to use this approach. Opportunities are given to listen to interpersonal transactions and evaluate how costly they may be in terms of a relationship, then suggesting more effective ways to relate. These examples are excellent and provide an opportunity to transfer the theory into practice.

The focus of the book, then, is on human relations and communication. It provides the reader with an opportunity to not only develop a more empathic attitude but to acquire some of the skills essential for "keeping in touch."

DON DINKMEYER, PH.D.

President, Communication &
Motivation Training Institute
Coral Springs, FL. 33065

Preface

Seldom are we afforded the opportunity to analyze our interpersonal communication systems. It seems true that even as concerned members of our society, we do not voluntarily scrutinize the effects of our communication styles.

This book is written with the belief that we can now determine the effective, as well as the ineffective, ingredients in interpersonal communication. Described in the pages of *Keep in Touch* are the often unrecognized obstacles in communication that affect such important facets of our society as productivity, motivation, morale, enthusiasm, credibility, and the like. Disregarding these obstacles will adversely affect the development of personalities and attitudes, especially within families, schools, and businesses.

No author can control the impact of his or her writing on an individual or a society. However, this book is designed to help people in all walks of life to establish better relationships. The material is presented with the intention of bringing human relations skills to the general public, but it is void of educational and psychological jargon.

Acquisition of these communication skills can assist people in building a personally effective system of communication that will promote better relationships. The skills help to rid ourselves of the ineffective, archaic, autocratic approach individuals often use with each other and assist us in developing a more democratic attitude. We can do it!

The materials and ideas of others interested in improving the quality of life in our society have been used throughout the book. I would gratefully like to acknowledge the use of material derived from the *Chicago Tribune, WBBM-TV Channel 2 in Chicago* (TV series entitled "Project Parenting"), *United Press International* and Rabbi Maurice Davis of the Reform Synagogue in White Plains, New York. I would also like to thank Janet Murrow for permission to use her late husband's words in an epigraph.

Please note: Since there is no neutral pronoun in the singular, "he" or "she" is often used to eliminate any sexual bias. Constant, repetitive use of such expressions is distracting and on occasion "he," "him," "his," or "himself" is used to include both sexes.

Acknowledgments

The inspiration to write this book came to me after I had organized and then taught several classes on interpersonal communication. It was during this time that I realized the profound effect my professors had on me. It is a humble notation when I mention how indebted I am to the skillful teaching of Dr. Grady Harlan, Department Chairman, and Dr. Dudley Sykes, Dr. F. J. Eicke, and Dr. Phil Cooker, professors in the Department of Counseling and Educational Psychology at the University of Mississippi. This book could not have been written without the knowledge they passed my way. My sincere hope is that the book is an accurate reflection of their teaching efforts.

A very important contribution was made by R. A. Keenan, whose expertise gave the book clarity and, undoubtedly, made it publishable. To her I am indeed grateful. Sincere thanks are extended to my friends Marc Denny, Charles Gaharan, Bill Schultz, and Jim Spengler, who made valuable corrections and additions as did Bennie Smith, copyeditor. Their work is acknowledged and appreciated. I would also like to thank Jan Bone and Dr. William Walsh, fellow authors, for their valuable assistance. The guiding hands of Betty Neville in the permissions department, Lynne Lumsden, Senior Editor of Spectrum Books, and Claire Verduin, Editor, Brooks/Cole Publishing Company, did not go unnoticed. I found these individuals to be very human, and I wish to express my gratitude for the direction they provided. A sincere acknowledgment is directed toward my brother, Wendell, for all of his leg work and encouragement during the construction of the manuscript.

During the writing process I coaxed, pleaded, and even coerced many of my friends, colleagues, neighbors, and relatives into careful scrutiny of the book. It is impossible to acknowledge all of them, except in a group "thank you," but their feedback was vital to the contents.

This book is dedicated to my instructors, friends, and colleagues,
my wife, Pat, and my three daughters, Denise, Diane, and Debbie,
all of whom helped give me the inspiration to finish this project.
May we always strive "to keep in touch."

NORM JONES

one

The Culprit LLPs!

Before he died, Dr. Martin Luther King, Jr. said, "People don't know each other because they have not properly communicated with each other." Dr. King recognized that speaking with one another does not ensure proper communication.

A great deal of time and money are spent on ecology and pollution control, interstate highways, space ventures, and legal battles in the courtroom, but not much time or money is spent to improve interpersonal communication, which can be vital to success in business, marriage, parenting, education, and even international summit meetings! The quality of communication with which we are involved affects us deeply and directly. Thus, the need for "proper" communication, as Dr. King called it, would be of great concern to anyone interacting with other people—that is, to each and every one of us!

Indeed, many parents, teachers, students, businesspersons, nurses, counselors, and so on, do realize that they could benefit in their careers and daily lives by improving their interpersonal communication skills. Yet a number of these people agonize when they attempt a new system of communication. There seems to be a natural inclination to resist change even though it can readily be seen that the change is for the better. It is easier to continue using the response patterns and listening habits that have become deeply rooted in us throughout our lives than it is to attempt to change them. Life Long Patterns of ineffective interpersonal responses have actually been ingrained into our personalities by other people in our lives and reinforced through daily use. It is understandable, then, that after the firm establishment of our Life Long Patterns (LLPs) most of us experience difficulty when trying to incorporate new response patterns into our lives.

However, the change *can* be effected, and there appears to be a need today to examine our communication techniques to see if it is, indeed, time for change. Many parents, for example, have not had anyone help them recognize their ineffective, ingrained ways of talking with their children. Consequently, family problems have often resulted. The same holds true for teachers and their students.

Surprisingly, current research studies indicate that even those people who have received advanced training in psychology, human relations, counseling, and therapy and are practitioners in the helping professions, are actually not very helpful. One such study reveals that 70 percent of the Roman Catholic priests were "underdeveloped" in interpersonal skills and were, in fact, "ordinary men" (Egan, 1975) when assessed as to their helping skills. Another study found that the average counselor was a "low-level helper." Research infers that such helping professions as the ministry, social work, psychiatry, counseling, and teaching, as well as psychology and law, are usually staffed with people whose skills in the helping process rate low (Egan 1975). An additional study indicated that "helping persons" unintentionally caused clients to become dependent on them. Other studies have shown similar results.

Respecting this research, consider how often we hear that a friend or neighbor has visited a helper, such as a psychologist, and has come away saying, "It was a waste of time and money," or "He didn't help me a bit."

The research is mentioned because I believe that LLPs, the deeply rooted communication patterns previously alluded to, are the crux of many problems, not only in the psychological professions, but in our families, schools, and businesses. It makes little difference whether we are talking about ineffective relationships between a parent and a child, a teacher and student, psychologist and client, or businesspersons and their customers. LLPs are often the culprit! The need for change is present!

LLPs Exposed

The transition from LLPs to improved response patterns, while necessitating effort and concentration, need not be feared. The Life Long Patterns can be ferreted out! Once recognized, they can be evaluated and then refined into a more effective system. This book is designed to help you make this change with the hope that the end result will be confidence in a personally effective system of communication that will promote better relationships.

With some willingness to take a good look at ourselves, we can improve our communications. We can rid ourselves of our deeply rooted patterns and hear the words people say in a new, more meaningful, *feeling* way. This newly acquired skill will automatically clarify the messages we send and receive. The information in this book can help if you want to change, but you must be ready to perceive yourself differently. If you are able to look into yourself and see communication techniques you would like to change, then I suggest you no longer leave the possibility of problems creeping into your marriage, business, friendship, and so on, to chance. Learning and implementing new interpersonal skills can increase the probability of better relationships over a long period of time. Reading about and then experiencing change from LLPs is a small price to pay for personal growth.

First, a word of caution. If, in the course of reading about LLPs, you say to yourself, "Yep, that's describing me all right," don't become fearful that this experience is going to be an encounter of the worst kind. People to whom I've taught these skills have convinced me that they *must* agonize a little with themselves before they really recognize LLPs and begin work to eliminate them from their communication techniques. For most people it seems difficult to look at themselves in an introspective way. As they read examples of conversations where LLPs are preventing effective responses, they may become painfully aware of similarities to their own in which they failed to respond to the *feelings* of the other person involved.

Such self-accusation is certainly unnecessary and undesirable. One should not lose sight of the true origin of our Life Long Patterns. They have developed through generations in that they include value systems, judgments, morality, work ethics, and so forth, that have been passed overtly or covertly from age to age. In our own lifetimes our personal communication patterns have been further shaped by our interaction with parents, teachers, clergy, classmates, friends . . . the sum total of acquaintances, experiences, traditions, and heredity. No individual should take all the credit or all the blame when he or she looks in the mirror!

Without a doubt the most difficult obstacle to overcome in learning new interpersonal communication skills is the removal of our "ingrained selves," our frame of references, our prejudices, our life experiences, our judgments, our solutions, our advice and assumptions from the world of another human being. It is just such elements as these that make up our LLPs. I'm sure that to many readers asking for the elimination, or at least a reduction of these elements from the conversations we have, leads them to say, "Am I to act like I'm nobody and let others do whatever they please to me?" Or, as one teacher said in a training session, "Are we just to be bland?" Please grasp the book a little more firmly and read on! That which I am about to describe does not help weaken people, but serves to strengthen them.

Responding to the Feeling

I have learned that our LLPs run so deeply within us that we must "start from scratch" to rid ourselves of them. The first step is to learn to respond to the *feeling* someone is expressing instead of responding to an *event* or *situation.* In teaching this skill, my first objective is to show people how to get themselves out of the way so they can respond to the other person's feelings rather than to their own LLPs. Too many people who attempt to help another actually impose *their* solutions on the other person's difficulties. They cannot remove themselves and just listen, thereby assisting the other person to help himself. They have to tell the individual what to do, or talk in such a way that the person knows they are really prescribing a program for him to follow. Dependence on the helping person often develops and the troubled person is soon unable to depend on himself to work out life's difficulties. We should work from the premise that if we want to help someone develop, we must not get in the way of that development. We must conscientiously attempt to set aside our ingrained responses and concentrate on the feelings of the person speaking.

It is an awkward experience at first, a trying one at best, but one that is very rewarding when people know they are able to "get themselves out of the way" and actually respond to the feelings of someone else.

The usual response I hear after a few teaching sessions is, "I didn't realize I was so bad," or "I can see what I have to do now," or "I knew I could do better, but I wasn't sure how," or even, "I need this stuff so much."

An example is needed here so the reader can begin to experience the awareness of LLPs. Following is a typical case where the father of a boy, reacting to his own value system, responded to an *event* rather than to his son's real *feelings*.

The father called me, the boy's counselor, and asked if I had any insight into why his son's grades slipped into Cs from Bs during the last grading period. I said I had heard nothing from his teachers or his son, but I would be glad to investigate the matter. I began my investigation right there on the telephone. I received some possible clues from the father as I was talking with him. Since I firmly believe that poor communication is often the source of many of life's problems, I asked the father what he had said to the boy when he had first received the Bs. The father said, "I told him they were good, to keep up the good work and that grades are important." The father and I agreed that what he had said was a common, rather typical response. I then asked the father what he said when the boy delivered the Cs to him. The father told me he said something like, "Your grades have gone down. Aren't you working? You know how important grades are!" Realizing LLPs could be part of the problem I asked the father if he could arrange to spend an hour or so with me. He agreed.

During our conference I was successful in helping the father to expose his LLPs and to assist him in understanding why it is important in human relations to respond to *feelings* rather than to an event. I began the conference by explaining that there could be numerous reasons why his son's grades had slipped, but my primary reason for asking the father to come into my office was to *prevent* further problems between him and his boy over grades and, more than likely to prevent increasing tension between father and son. I thought that if this father could relate just a little better to his son, the boy would *more likely* do the best he could in school. If tension started building over grades, the boy might not be able to perform at his best level.

I mentioned to the father that quite possibly his *first* comment about the B grades "being good" was the beginning of what could be a partial solution to the problem. I explained by first recalling his statement, "That's good, keep up the good work, grades are important," that he was projecting a great deal of himself into the event and could hinder his son's growth. I explained that he was coming from *his* frame of reference, *his* value system, *his* experiences in life, *his* background, and was not responding to his son's feelings about his school work. He was spending the communication time talking about *his* own feelings rather than about his boy's feelings. I further explained that research seems to be telling us that if we respond to the feelings of people, we can start to build a relationship with them; we can "get with them" much easier. They will trust us more and feel freer to discuss problems and talk about themselves. They can grow! If we keep heaping our "stuff" on them, they will withdraw from us. Paying more attention to the words people say rather than their feeling will not promote relationships, but will serve to limit them. As S. I. Hayakawa once said, "The meanings of words are not in the words, they are in us" (Banville, 1978, p. 11).

I told the father that *some* praise, such as he had been giving, is needed and often appropriate. However, the ability to pick up feeling, exact feeling, is just as important. The father said, "I understand what you are saying, but how do I do it?" I reiterated we must first learn to remove our ingrained selves more than we currently do. We must not let ourselves get in the way so much. We simply do not perceive an event the same way as someone else, and we cannot expect them to identify with our perceptions of it. We must key into their sensitivities.

In order to give the father an example of more feeling type responses I suggested something like, "You seem to be proud of what you accomplished at school." The father recalled that the boy was, indeed, smiling when they first discussed the Bs and did seem very proud. I suggested that he respond to the smile and proud feeling his boy was giving him instead of something of his own that the boy could not relate to as well. I explained that when someone expresses some feeling to us we "should go with that feeling" rather than with something *we* feel. I further explained that our feelings are important, but we must learn to understand the deep feelings of others to establish good relationships.

I asked the father if he was now aware of what I meant when I said that we must first learn to remove our LLPs from the communication process? I also asked if he could now see that he responded to the event (a report card) instead of the feeling (the boy's pride in the Bs)? The father said yes, but asked me why we haven't been able to respond correctly and remove the so-called LLPs? I answered by saying that we learn response patterns from our parents and teachers and other significant adults in our lives while we are growing up. The system becomes firmly fixed within us and is difficult to change. All of us respond in a similar fashion to people around us every day of our lives. We *think* we know ourselves, and because of this belief, we think we know others and what is best for them (Banville, 1978).

LLPs are something we must recognize in ourselves and then be willing to replace with a new response system. We must realize that we are the ones who must change instead of trying to change those around us. We simply spend too much time trying to change things in other people that we are often responsible for in the first place.

With some knowledge of current research and years of observation in the public schools, I now believe the inability to ferret out feeling is the major cause of ill feelings between students and teachers, parents and children, husbands and wives, and employers and employees.

Some authorities contend that such "feelingless" responses tend to generate resentment between people. I mentioned to the father that one of the things we do when we respond in such a "feelingless" way is take away a small opportunity for the kids to grow. And then we so often say to them, "Grow up!" This is double jeopardy!

The father left my office and said he would go to work on the problem. But that bothered me somewhat because I knew the father had not learned a more effective way of responding in the hour we had spent together. I recommended some reading for him, but cautioned him that changing his current method of responding was something he would have to spend some time on. The change would be something he must *experience* in many different situations before he could become very proficient at responding better.

Since the meeting with the father, I have concentrated my efforts in helping people by first looking at their methods of communication. My major thrust is to teach them to discover feelings being relayed to them from other people and to become better listeners. An attempt is made to assist them in recognizing the difference between idle conversation and communication involving feelings. These people are encouraged to respond to pleasant and unpleasant states of life "coming from the other person" rather than always coming from themselves. Explained to these people is the idea that we can develop an ability to *hear feeling* and respond to it. We are not learning how to become counselors during this time. We are learning to pick up feeling and work with it in a more effective manner.

Getting Out of the Way

"Are you coming from yourself?" is a favorite expression of mine during class sessions. I think it is important, in undertaking this change process, for all of us to understand the concept of "removing ourselves" or "phasing ourselves out." Once we understand exactly what is meant by that we can begin to make changes that most tell me are very rewarding.

Practicing recognition of feeling is the process whereby people begin to recognize their typical LLPs. Doing so is very awkward for most people in the first few sessions of a class or seminar and often people disagree with the new concept for at least the first thirty minutes. Some simply don't return for a second session while others catch on quickly.

Examples of LLPs

In the first session the participants in the classes are given examples of conversations which emote some human feeling. They are then asked to write their responses. For example, they are asked to pretend that someone says the following examples to them and they are instructed to write their responses:

Example 1. I've felt terrible all week. All the other kids in school belong to their own groups, but not me. I don't think they like me. I don't know why.

Example 2. Wow, have I got it going. My English teacher told me I got an A on my theme and just today I made the basketball team.

After a brief period of time the class members are asked to check their responses and see if they responded to feeling they recognized in each speaker. I usually ask such questions as: "What kind of "feeling word" did you use in your response?" "Did you *really* identify the feeling being expressed?" I remind the class that research infers that it is important to respond to the feeling rather than the event. "Were you able to get yourselves out of the way?" is another question that seems to have some meaning to them.

One father, when asked to respond to Example 1, said he needed to know if he was talking to his son or daughter, as he and his daughter were relating well, but he and his son were not. This told me that he would make a different response according to whom he was talking. Yet the example could be said by either a boy or a girl. The father understood that he was not yet able to "get himself out of the way" in talking with his kids. While working with a counselor, I pointed out that he gave himself away when he said to a student, "I'm glad you think your decision is a good one too!" In both cases LLPs were still present. The father and counselor had devised "programs" for each youngster and were responding in such a way to put their programs into effect. They were passing over the feelings being emitted by the young people.

Other class members also had difficulty relating to feeling. Though believing they were doing so, most could not write down a response that reflected any feeling. Following are typical replies to Example 1 that were made by beginning class members:

Just forget about them. There are plenty of other kids at school and in the neighborhood.

Stop feeling sorry for yourself! That is what they want you to do. Don't let them get to you.

You are probably trying too hard. Just be yourself. They will let you in soon.

Don't worry about it! You will find new pals in time.

Just try to be nicer. Kids can be very cruel sometimes. Things will change.

Do you really think they feel that way about you?

You must take the first step. Have you invited them to do anything?

As you can see, no feeling word is used in these very typical responses. No feeling is alluded to. It is reasonably clear in Example 1 that the person feels left out, excluded, alone, rejected, or abandoned, or some such "feeling word" closely related to these words. A better response would be, "You feel left out and no matter how hard you try nothing seems to be working for you right now."

In my view, this statement at least lets the individual know the listener heard what was said. The listener did not respond from his or her past history or own frame of reference. He has communicated some feeling and understanding and has not detracted from what the person said to him.

Dr. Michael Lillibridge (1977) skillfully addresses himself to this problem in listening on his Interpersonal Communication Skills tape series. He suggests that there are two main ways to communicate. One is expressed in words, and the other is expressed in feeling or intention. Dr. Lillibridge suggests that we should attempt to make words and feeling coincide when we communicate. We should become more able to say just how we feel and also try to understand how the people we address actually feel. If what is expressed in words correlates very highly with what is felt, there is a good chance that meaningful communication will occur. Once people feel they are being understood, they are more apt to take constructive action on their own behalf. If they know they have been listened to carefully, they may want to accept a suggestion. If people know they aren't being listened to, it gives them little faith in others and their suggestions or advice (Lillibridge, 1977).

A response such as "You feel left out, and no matter how hard you try nothing seems to be working for you," reflects the feeling of being left out or excluded. The person being left out can now come closer to putting the intended feeling into words. Please notice in Example 1 that the individual did not *say* he felt left out or excluded. If this individual doesn't have his feelings clarified by others in his life, he will very possibly act on feelings that he does not understand. He can only understand himself in direct correlation to what other people help him to understand about himself.

After practice periods have revealed some of the rather typical responses and everyone in the group has become aware that there is a better way to communicate, they quickly acquire what I call "apparent insight" into this new experience in communications. The next step is to help them refine their skills and incorporate them into their daily lives.

Rules

I have formulated a set of rules which forces people to respond differently provided they abide by the rules. Please read and try to remember as many of them as you can as you read the remainder of the book.

1. Take the feeling, not the event.
2. Use a feeling word. Don't minimize feelings.
3. Eliminate questions!
4. Eliminate logic and assumptions.
5. Don't send solutions or give advice.
6. Allow them to do the talking.
7. Eliminate evaluations, opinions, judgments, and analysis.

As you might surmise, these rules cannot be taken as absolutes, but they should be regarded as such in the *early* stages of learning these new response patterns and adhered to more often in our daily relationships.

After the rules have been distributed to everyone in the group, I ask them to use the rules they just received and to again write down a response to Example 1. During one particular session, a father spoke out after having studied the rules and said, "You have just eliminated the possibility of me ever talking to anyone again." The class and I laughed, but it is that type of feeling people must have if they are going to have any chance of learning how to respond more effectively.

It is very common for participants in a class or workshop to take several minutes just to make a simple response that includes all the rules. Spontaneity is forgotten! With practice, however, most people can incorporate the rules and new responses and regain spontaneity.

Of course, the rules are specifically designed to assist people in dissolving their LLPs. Rule 1 should sound familiar. It was this rule, and the reasons for it, that was illustrated when class members were made aware of their LLPs by writing their results. Its importance was also seen in the case where the father responded to his son's report card rather than to his son's feelings about the report card.

Reacting to the feeling rather than the event is the first step in recognizing our ingrained habits, but the other rules are equally important. As they are discussed throughout the chapters, their usefulness will become apparent.

The suggested response to Example 1 (You feel left out, and no matter how hard you try nothing seems to be working for you) follows *all* of the rules as did the response to the boy who brought home all Bs on his report card (You seem to be proud of what you accomplished at school). It does take time to learn this new system, but after four or five class meetings most people have enough insight that if they faithfully continue to practice and use the rules, they can make the new technique a part of their communication system.

I have found that when the rules are conscientiously applied in practice sessions either in or out of class it is then people actually begin to recognize the ineffective, deeply rooted communication system most of us have within us. They become more aware that the interpersonal skill of listening for and identifying feeling is not usually an inherited trait, but, in fact, must be developed. This skill is not natural in our society, but can and should be learned.

After following the suggested rules and other ideas for a substantial length of time, most people discover they have learned to listen to themselves more closely. They have begun to understand just how often, how *very* often, they hinder the growth of another because "they get in the way." They are now able to understand how they get in the other person's court and "take the ball away from them." They understand how LLPs affect relationships.

I am curious and very interested in how readers are doing at this point in the book. Are you perceiving yourself differently? If you have had some sort of strange feeling come over you, I would hope it would be that you can see a change you would like to make in your life and that you will join those who have some apparent insight and can muster enough courage to go forward.

There is little doubt in my mind that my groups have taught me as much about human behavior as I have taught them about communication skills. I have discovered, for example, that people can get themselves out of the way in a relatively short period of time, but they need more help in addressing themselves to deep feeling. They tend to use general, rather than specific, feeling words. One of the more common responses used in early practice sessions is, "It sounds like you are unhappy." Being unhappy is a general feeling. We become "unhappy" about a lot of things. If a youngster says to us, "They always choose me last! I know I'm not very good, but I do like to play. They never, never let me! What can I do about it?" we should learn to become more specific with the feeling words if we are to help clarify feelings. The youngster *is* unhappy, but more specifically, he or she has been overlooked, offended, cast off, alienated, or excluded. A great deal of practice is needed to refine the technique of using specific feeling words. On the other hand, general feeling words are certainly more acceptable than some of the "stuff" we are accustomed to firing back.

At any rate, I encourage people to try and use the best feeling words they can think of when responding. People try hard, but when I check their responses they invariably leave out a good, strong feeling word. Because of this I have found it beneficial to distribute the following list of feeling words. They are words very common to our society. They are all found in the dictionary and all describe some feeling or human emotion. Please look over the list and notice that you know the meaning of the words, but you do not often hear or use them when talking with people. The list should give a clue as to why research infers that feeling is not picked up as readily as it should be in our daily communication.

Obviously, the list is designed to help the user develop a more descriptive vocabulary of "feeling words." Becoming familiar with many of these words will be essential in applying them at the right moment in everyday living. Most of the words we know rather well, but we must teach ourselves to use them more often in responding to others' feelings.

Why, you might ask, are these words so important in communicating? Experts in interpersonal communication believe that people

PLEASANT AFFECTIVE STATES

Love, Affection, Concern

admired	dedicated	just	receptive
adorable	devoted	kind	reliable
affectionate	easygoing	kindly	respectful
agreeable	empathetic	kindhearted	responsible
altruistic	fair	lenient	sensitive
amiable	faithful	lovable	sympathetic
benevolent	forgiving	loving	sweet
benign	friendly	mellow	tender
bighearted	generous	mild	thoughtful
brotherly	genuine	moral	tolerant
caring	giving	neighborly	truthful
charitable	good	nice	trustworthy
Christian	good-hu-mored	obliging	understanding
comforting	good-natured	open	unselfish
congenial	helpful	optimistic	warm
conscientious	honest	patient	warmhearted
considerate	honorable	peaceful	well-meaning
cooperative	hospitable	pleasant	wise
cordial	humane	polite	
courteous	interested	reasonable	

Elation, Joy

amused	exalted	humorous	serene
at ease	excellent	inspired	splendid
blissful	excited	in high spirits	superb
brilliant	fantastic	jovial	terrific
calm	fine	joyful	thrilled
cheerful	fit	jubilant	tremendous
comical	gay	magnificent	triumphant
contented	glad	majestic	turned on
delighted	glorious	marvelous	vivacious
ecstatic	good	overjoyed	witty
elated	grand	pleased	wonderful
elevated	gratified	pleasant	
enchanted	great	proud	
enthusiastic	happy	satisfied	

Potency

able	durable	influential	spirited
adequate	dynamic	intense	stable
assured	effective	lionhearted	stouthearted

PLEASANT AFFECTIVE STATES *(Continued)*

Potency (Continued)

authoritative	energetic	manly	strong
bold	fearless	mighty	sure
brave	firm	powerful	tough
capable	forceful	robust	virile
competent	gallant	secure	well equipped
confident	hardy	self-confident	well put together
courageous	healthy	self-reliant	
daring	heroic	sharp	
determined	important	skillful	

Depression

abandoned	despised	horrible	pathetic
alien	despondent	humiliated	pitiful
alienated	destroyed	hurt	rebuked
alone	discarded	in the dumps	regretful
annihilate	discouraged	jilted	rejected
awful	disfavored	kaput	reprimanded
battered	dismal	left out	rotten
below par	done for	loathed	ruined
blue	downcast	lonely	rundown
burned	downhearted	lonesome	sad
cast off	downtrodden	lousy	stranded
cheapened	dreadful	low	tearful
crushed	estranged	miserable	terrible
debased	excluded	mishandled	unhappy
defeated	forlorn	mistreated	unloved
degraded	forsaken	moody	valueless
dejected	gloomy	mournful	washed up
demolished	glum	obsolete	whipped
depressed	grim	ostracized	worthless
desolate	hated	out of sorts	wrecked

Distress

afflicted	displeased	lost	swamped
anguished	dissatisfied	nauseated	the plaything of
at the feet of	distrustful	offended	the puppet of
at the mercy of	disturbed	pained	tormented
awkward	doubtful	perplexed	tough
baffled	foolish	puzzled	ungainly
bewildered	futile	ridiculous	unlucky
blameworthy	grief	sickened	unpopular
clumsy	helpless	silly	unsatisfied
confused	hindered	skeptical	unsure
constrained	impaired	speechless	
disgusted	impatient	strained	
disliked	imprisoned	suspicious	

PLEASANT AFFECTIVE STATES *(Continued)*

Fear, Anxiety

afraid	fearful	jittery	shy
agitated	fidgety	jumpy	strained
alarmed	frightened	nervous	tense
anxious	hesitant	on edge	terrified
apprehensive	horrified	overwhelmed	terror-stricken
bashful	ill at ease	panicky	timid
desperate	insecure	restless	uncomfortable
dread	intimidated	scared	uneasy
embarrassed	jealous	shaky	

Belittling, Criticism, Scorn

abused	diminished	maligned	scoffed at
belittled	discredited	minimized	scorned
branded	disdained	mocked	shamed
carped at	disgraced	neglected	slammed
caviled at	disparaged	not taken seriously	slandered
censured	humiliated	overlooked	slighted
criticized	ignored	poked fun at	thought nothing of
defamed	jeered	pooh-poohed	underestimated
deprecated	laughed at	put down	underrated
depreciated	libeled	ridiculed	
derided	made light of	roasted	

Impotency, Inadequacy

anemic	flimsy	insecure	unable
broken	fragile	insufficient	unarmed
broken down	frail	lame	uncertain
chickenhearted	harmless	maimed	unfit
cowardly	helpless	meek	unimportant
crippled	impotent	nerveless	unqualified
debilitated	inadequate	paralyzed	unsound
defective	incapable	powerless	unsubstantiated
deficient	incompetent	puny	useless
demoralized	indefensible	shaken	vulnerable
disabled	ineffective	shaky	weak
effeminate	inefficient	sickly	weak-hearted
exhausted	inept	small	
exposed	inferior	strengthless	
feeble	infirm	trivial	

Anger, Hostility, Cruelty

agitated	antagonistic	bigoted	callous
aggravated	arrogant	biting	cold-blooded

Anger, Hostility, Cruelty (Continued)

aggressive	austere	bloodthirsty	combative
angry	bad-tem- pered	blunt	contankerous
annoyed	beligerent	bullying	contrary
cool	hardhearted	malicious	rude
corrosive	harsh	mean	ruthless
cranky	hateful	murderous	sadistic
critical	heartless	nasty	savage
cross	hellish	obstinate	severe
cruel	hideous	opposed	spiteful
deadly	hostile	oppressive	stern
dictatorial	hypercritical	outraged	stormy
disagreeable	ill-tempered	perturbed	unfeeling
discontented	impatient	poisonous	unfriendly
dogmatic	inconsiderate	prejudiced	unmerciful
enraged	inhuman	pushy	unruly
envious	insensitive	rebellious	vicious
fierce	intolerable	reckless	vindictive
furious	intolerant	resentful	violent
gruesome	irritated	revengeful	wrathful
hard	mad	rough	

who have feelings reflected back to them can spend the next instant contemplating their feelings and behavior. They do not have to rummage through someone's LLPs or begin wondering why they have not been listened to. If their feelings are not responded to, they have little evidence that real communication is taking place. If we just come close to hitting the right feeling word, even if it is inexact, individuals with whom we are talking can still let us know if they overstated or understated their feelings, or if we misinterpreted them.

Mutual understanding is more likely to take place when feelings are understood. An individual is more likely to reveal himself when his feelings are shared. Creditable psychologists or psychiatrists know that they alone do not work out solutions to problems people encounter; they assist people in working out their difficulties.

A great deal of anxiety is "free-floating" fear, a fear of something unidentified. If we respond to the feelings people express to us, we may help them to identify fears or sources of nervousness, and once identified, the anxiety may subside. At least then they can begin to deal with it; they can't deal with it if they don't know what it is!

We must understand that we can learn a great deal more about a person if he or she discusses feelings freely. If engaged and married couples would more readily adopt this technique, their relationships would vastly improve and the divorce rate, doubled since 1968 in our country, might decline.

Discussing feelings freely and openly is one of the primary ingredients of successful therapy. It allows people an emotional discharge which in turn will allow them to better understand themselves.[1] When psychoanalysis or therapy is helpful, it is because someone is able to respond to the deep feelings of another. Be assured that effective therapists realize the importance of "allowing the other person to do the talking" so they can pick up the person's feelings.

In their book *Beyond Counseling and Therapy* (1967), Carkhuff and Berenson speak about "helping someone to experience himself." We can do this by learning to respond to deep feelings, by using more feeling words. At the same time we might keep in mind that people develop as a result of the feelings they continually witness within themselves.

Picking Up Feeling

We should consider the fact that people very often fail to use the proper word to describe their feelings. Recall the boy who was *proud* of his report card and the youngster who seemed to be *left out, excluded* or *alone*. If we just listen to people we will hear a lot of feeling, but few words on the feeling word list are actually used by those sending out the feeling. We don't seem to use those words to respond to feeling, and we aren't very good about using them to explain our innermost feelings. And unheard feelings, those feelings kept inside of us, can cause ailments such as tension, ulcers, headaches, or, projected over a long period of time, unhealthy life styles. Yes, clinging to our LLPs, our poor communication techniques, can cause many of the above ailments!

[1] From *BEYOND COUNSELING AND THERAPY* by Robert R. Carkhuff and Bernard G. Berenson. Copyright © 1967 by Holt, Rinehart and Winston, Inc. Reprinted by permission of Holt, Rinehart and Winston.

Why is it we can fine tune our color TV sets, our CBs, our stereos, our ICBMs, but not ourselves? We must first listen to ourselves as we communicate real feeling to someone. To do so brings about self-awareness. Listening to ourselves can help tell us what *we* are really feeling and what we are really saying in terms of feeling without using a feeling word to describe it.

Another point to remember when picking up feeling is that positive feelings must be responded to as well as negative or unpleasant feelings. That is the reason the feeling word list has both pleasant and unpleasant terms. Positive feelings are easy, in most respects, to recognize, but can be difficult to handle, difficult to respond to with a feeling word.

Let's hypothesize that a teacher friend of yours says, "I'm so pleased with my class. They are working well together. Recently it has been a real joy to teach. I have a great deal of energy and look forward to each day. Compared to last semester it's like night and day!" Obviously, this teacher is elated, contented, pleased, gratified, inspired, and/or satisfied. To allow her to enjoy her good feeling and let her know we heard her, we could respond with, "Well, I get the impression you are satisfied with your work and are inspired to keep going." Now I realize close friends may tease each other once in a while and pull what might be called a "Don Rickles" by saying something like, "Keep going, things will get worse, they always do." Very often this comes across as funny, and Don Rickles has refined this type of response into something very funny. However, there are times when positive feelings should be reinforced, but they usually are not. For example, when our children are excited, we can teach ourselves to pick up their excitement and respond to it. If your son or daughter comes home and says in an excited voice, "I scored nine points in the volleyball game and made the winning points," we should not respond with, "That's good! Now please, let me watch the news." I realize most of us don't respond that poorly, but we often say things like, "That's great! Did you play the whole game?" Or, "Did Diane get to play this week?" How far off is this response from one containing the feeling of pride, or being thrilled or delighted? Even if a friend says, "I'm so excited, I'm going to Hawaii for two weeks!", we often "dampen" the excitement by saying something like, "The last time I was in Hawaii it rained every day!"

We respond in such "feelingless" ways much of the time. We

minimize feelings, especially positive feelings. It is almost as though we have difficulty enjoying someone's enjoyment!

Let's look more closely at the above response between father and son or daughter. How many of our rules were broken? Yes, most of them were at least bent a little. The person responded to the event instead of feeling. The father left out a feeling word, started asking questions, and did not respond in such a way that the person could continue to talk about his or her good feelings. Saying, "That's great," is not so terrible, but it becomes so if we respond in such an evaluative way all the time to the same person. It can become a dangerous LLP!

It is human nature to want to let other people know how good or bad we feel. Youngsters certainly want and need to let adults know how they feel. If we don't respond to feelings early in their lives, they will not be willing to share with us later. Often, young people seek a better existence, which to them may be drugs or alcohol or even running away. An individual cannot reject the openness the youngsters are expressing and develop a loving relationship. We reject openness and love when we fail to respond to feeling (Banville, 1978).

Let's take a look at one other example of "minimizing." When I began lecturing and teaching about interpersonal communication skills, I was quite excited about my newly acquired skill to help people develop their communication techniques. I had received some good feedback. One day I said to a friend, "Well, I'm a little excited because this Friday morning I am delivering my first lecture. I'm going to talk to a group of teachers and make some extra spending money." My friend said, "Don't forget how far behind you get when you are out of the office." All of a sudden my excitement was gone! My colleague did not share my positive feelings. I gave out more feeling than was acknowledged. A better response might have been, "You have found something you really enjoy doing and to get paid for it makes it all the more exciting." I guess I would like to have heard my suggested response, but I understood the LLP and shrugged it off. I think this example points out that very often when we forget to respond to feelings, the final result of a conversation is not necessarily the intended one.

In an inspiring book entitled *Who Will Listen?*, Dr. Clark Moustakas wrote, "Learning to listen and to hear, learning to respond to others in a way that respects and encourages them, are essential experiences in the growth of a relationship" (Moustakas, 1975, p. 2). Clearly, our personalities develop as a result of our LLPs. The next chapter examines some of the reasons *why* our LLPs prevent us from picking up feeling and why we often respond in discouraging ways. We will look at why our LLPs usually don't afford us the ability to respond to feeling and why relationships begin breaking down.

References

BANVILLE, THOMAS G. *How to Listen—How to Be Heard.* Chicago: Nelson-Hall, 1978.

CARKHUFF, ROBERT R. and BERENSON, BERNARD G. *Beyond Counseling and Therapy.* New York: Holt, Rinehart and Winston, Inc., 1967.

EGAN, G. *The Skilled Helper.* Monterey, California: Brooks/Cole Publishing Company, 1975.

GAZDA, G. M. *et. al. Human Relations Development: A Manual for Educators.* Boston: Copyright (c) 1973 by Allyn and Bacon, Inc.

LILLIBRIDGE, MICHAEL E. and KLUKKEN, GARY. *Interpersonal Communication Skills,* Cassette Tape Series, Affective House, Tulsa, Oklahoma, 1977.

MOUSTAKAS, C. *Who Will Listen?* New York: Ballantine Books (A Division of Random House), 1975

two

Let's Give It a Try

In the first chapter a great amount of space was devoted to convincing the reader of the importance of exposing deeply rooted methods of poor communication. We first had to learn how to deal with our LLPs and remove ourselves from the communication process, and insert a new, somewhat changed, person. We learned the importance of responding to feelings rather than events. We were introduced to the importance of "keeping the ball with the other person" (Gordon, 1970), so the individual would talk and better understand his or her feelings and so develop in a healthy psychological atmosphere. Examples were given, along with rules and word lists. All of this was only the beginning to mastering effective communication.

This chapter and the next center around those obstacles that prevent many of us from incorporating obviously needed changes in our communication systems. What *causes* us to miss the feeling another person is sending us? If we can understand why we miss it, we can learn to respond to it much more frequently and more accurately.

Our *illogical* use of logic is very often at the root of the breaking down of our interpersonal communications. (Please notice this is rule 4.) Logic is defined as "sound sense" or a "correct or reliable inference." A teacher attempts to use her logic in the following example:

A student says to her, "I just don't get this stuff. It's not making sense! Am I too dumb or something?" The teacher responds with what, for her, seems to be sound sense or a reliable inference when she says, "No, you aren't dumb; perhaps you just need to study more." By responding to the event rather than feeling, the teacher allows her *logical* solution ("study more") to prevent her from showing the student understanding, encouragement, and acceptance. Cued by the event and her LLPs the teacher starts applying her faulty logic because she *thinks* she has been in the same situation once and more study paid off for her. Unfortunately, we all tend to see the other's world as we have experienced our world (Shertzer and Stone, 1976). We tend to use logic this way: that it is something that has worked for us most every time and it should therefore work for everyone else. It doesn't!

The illogical use of logic in this case is that the teacher responded with something that is very often the reason for "not getting the stuff." Studying may be the solution, but if it isn't, the relationship suffers. Recall that research infers that we must respond to feeling in order to establish meaningful relationships. We simply cannot use logic, our logic, to change behavior! The teacher in this last example, as all teachers, would like to see the student learn "the stuff." However her faulty use of logic, at least in the beginning of the relationship, will only serve to tell the student, "My teacher wasn't listening," or "I better not comment again because I have been spending hours every night on this stuff and can't get it." It would be far better for the teacher to say something like, "You seem frustrated and are beginning to doubt your ability a little." Such a response removes logic and also helps us to follow all of the other rules.

Logic only allows an individual we are talking with to look at *our* solutions or revisions to problems. By responding to feeling, we can help a person look at *his* or *her* value system instead of ours. We should respond so the person can begin considering some possible revision, some alteration in his or her behavior, rather than dwelling on what we have hidden in our minds.

The use of logic, it seems, is such a big obstacle to hurdle that it had to be included in the rules. It is so big, in fact, that readers are encouraged to ask themselves as they respond to others, "Did I use logic, my logic, based upon my life experience, my frame of reference? Did I give some *sound sense* for the person I was talking with?" It more than likely won't do them any good. So forget what seems to be "sound sense" for you and work toward responding to the feeling level of a person.

Another way to eliminate the faulty use of logic is to remember that we should try to respond in such a way that we convey to someone that we really don't have a preconceived place in life where we would like for them to be. We should respond so we let people know that where *we* have been in life is not necessarily where *they* ought to go! We often respond with the idea in mind that our logic, our words, can force people to do things. We can't make anybody do anything! Not really!

We tend to respond with logic because we sometimes forget that the way we perceive things may be somewhat different from that of the person with whom we are talking. Our own perceptions may be very accurate; but if the other person's perceptions are inaccurate, we may unknowingly allow this confusion to prevent us from picking up feeling. The real feeling becomes somewhat distorted and the relationship suffers. Feelings are always right; facts producing feelings may be erroneous, but the feelings are right (Sugarman, 1978).

Many of my friends and colleagues know that one of my favorite expressions is, "We can't change behavior through the use of logic." I have verified this observation many times. I see many teachers and parents trying to use logic with little success.

I mentioned to a mother during a telephone conversation that she would find it very difficult to change her daughter's behavior through the use of logic. She said to me, "My God, what other way is there?" Well, as I hope you can now understand, the only way is to respond to people so they will *want* to change. They will want to change because, through clarification of their own feelings, their behavior becomes very clear to them and they decide to make a change.

On very limited occasions we may change behavior with logic or "sound sense." There are clues as to when logic is working and when it isn't. Dr. Michael Lillibridge, in his tape on listening skills, adheres to the notion that if a person starts to reject your ideas and argue with you, that is the time to stop, to listen again, and try to pick up some feeling (Lillibridge, 1977). Salespeople of all types have made this mistake in their selling techniques. I often hear salespeople push logic too far. The customers soon begin to feel that the salesperson doesn't really care about their needs, and thus the customers take their business elsewhere. The best salespeople are those who possess the skill to relate on a more empathetic level. Pushing logic, particularly when a great amount of feeling is involved, is a serious mistake in business.

Let's take a look at how pushing logic too far can be costly in the business world. Assume a middle-aged couple are being shown through a house by an agent from the Hardsell Real Estate Company. Assume the house has a bath and bedroom downstairs and a bath and three bedrooms upstairs. At the end of the tour the middle-aged lady says, "We like the house very much, but my father is going to be living with us and he has arthritis. I'm not sure he can combat the stairs." Many real estate agents respond with logic and say, "Possibly he could use the bath and bedroom downstairs." I maintain this is an error in communication. It does not help establish the credibility and trust that business people seem to agree is so important. First of all the agent's response *detracts* from the concern the lady has for her father. Secondly, it is a slight putdown when we tell someone the obvious such as "the bath and bedroom downstairs." The agent is using logic and persuasion in the wrong place. A better response might be, "Then the concern you have for your father is also an important factor in your buying a house." Responding in this manner, the agent is going "with the feeling" and not using logic to relate. This is just a good example of how overuse of logic may be costly. If the couple begins to distrust this agent they may take their business elsewhere. This is costly to the Hardsell Real Estate Company.

To further investigate our illogical use of logic, let's look again at the teacher/student example. When the teacher says "No, you aren't dumb. Perhaps you need to study more," and the student says "I've probably been coasting a little," the logic may be working. On the other hand if the student says "I don't see how I could spend any more time on this stuff. I study every night," it is clear that logic is not working. The teacher should then say something that reflects that student's feeling, such as "You have given a good effort, but are still discouraged," or "You know you have tried hard and are still feeling swamped." Many, however, continue with logic and say "Are you working or doing something else after school. Maybe that activity is interfering with school." Or possibly "You are spending too much time on other activities and not enough on school." Or even the popular "You can do it if you try. Your studies have to come first, so you may have to take more time."

The point I am making is this: if we establish a good listening relationship, a caring relationship in the beginning, our logic *may* be helpful in the future. Also, if a person doesn't accept our logic right away, we might just as well use this clue of nonacceptance and get back to the feeling we missed in the first place. If we persist with our logic, we are only going to make the individual resentful. Persisting with logic takes on the effect of a lecture. Students, children, and customers hear enough lectures! Parents, teachers, business people, all of us really, are too persistent with our use of logic in attempts to communicate.

Overuse of logic brings sad results. It is a tragic misuse of interpersonal power. Young people learn to keep their feelings from adults. They learn it is not very safe to share feelings with teachers, parents, and adults in general. When we hear young persons say "I don't want to talk about it," they are often just saying that they will get the adult logic, the adult version, heaped upon them; so it doesn't make any difference whether they talk or not. They are right!

Remember the example used earlier about the student who felt excluded? Some of the typical responses were as follows:

> Just forget about them. There are plenty of other kids at school and in the neighborhood.
> You are probably trying too hard. Just be yourself. They will let you in soon.
> Don't worry about it! You will find new pals in time.
> Just try to be nicer. Kids can be very cruel sometimes. Things will change.
> You must take the first step. Have you invited them to do anything?

All of these responses come from illogical use of logic. All responses sound like possible solutions. None contain the slightest bit of feeling.

Of course we would like to see the person be relieved of the misery, but we must keep in mind that the advice being given springs from logic, and we must remember that it is very difficult to change behavior through the use of logic. Most of the above responses urge the person to work out the problem or in some way feel better. It is almost like we, as listeners, have some magical quality which allows us to heal a person who is feeling left out or lonely. We don't!

In the case of the student who felt excluded, the words "Just try to be nicer," can come across as quite a blow, especially if the student has tried as much as possible "to be nice." We unknowingly use words to give young people verbal muggings. The use of logic can promote these muggings. We must become wary of its use!

Getting Started

Up to this point we have learned some rules to help us respond better and we have discovered that logic very often gets in our way. Once people understand the danger of carrying their logic too far in the communication process, they become somewhat confused as to how to respond and *not* use logic. Many people mention to me that if they apply most of the rules and eliminate logic, they can't find a way to begin a response. I think this is the usual experience and I try to help them learn skillful new ways to respond.

I usually begin by encouraging people to open a response with the word "You." It helps us to get ourselves out of the way by transferring the emphasis of the conversation immediately to the other person. So many of our LLPs start with "I," that teaching people to start a response with "you" is a good way to break the habit. When we start a response with "I" we are often well on the way to "putting our stuff on somebody." It is safer to start with "you" and we should make every effort to stay with that person's frame of reference when his or her feelings are involved.

After the word "you" is plugged into the response process, we add the word "feel." We practice for a few days responding to feelings we hear from people by beginning sentences with "You feel." This starter statement encourages people to respond to some feeling. For example, "You feel left out," is, in my opinion, a better response to the child being excluded from the group than "Don't worry about it, things will work out," or "Try to be nice and I'm sure they will let you in." I am hopeful readers can now realize the last two responses are less effective to helping an individual develop than the response "You feel left out," and may, in fact, be detrimental.

Individuals whom I have tried to teach these skills tell me the suggestion of "You feel" does seem to help them get started, and I then ask them to practice in their daily lives. I suggest that the reader also begin to practice by trying to respond to some feeling heard in his daily communication. Just say "You feel" once in a while when hearing feeling from someone. Leave out the event! For example, select a couple of words from the list on page fourteen. Let's say you choose "discouraged" and "excited." Now just wait until someone around you seems to be experiencing these feelings, and when they say something to you, just say "You feel discouraged," or "You feel excited about . . .!" Watch and see how the person reacts to you. Just practice plugging in "You feel" for a while. You will probably feel more uncomfortable than the person you are talking with, but you must experience this slight discomfort in order to progress and begin removing your LLPs.

The usual experience reported back to me is "I got started, but then I blew it." A humorous example was given to me by my brother. He stated that his son, a ninth grade student, presented him with his report card for the grading period. He tried to understand his son's feelings about his grades and said to him, "How do you feel about your grades?" His son said, "Well, I got an A, three Bs, and a C. Geometry is hard, but overall I think I'm pretty satisfied." My brother then said, "What can you do to make them better?" Sensing a lack of acknowledgement of his "pretty good" feelings, the boy brilliantly stated "Take easier classes!"

My brother and I had a good laugh over that exchange. He made a decent opening remark, hoping to get to his son's feelings, and then "blew it" with the second response (LLP). We have to train ourselves to hang in there longer and not allow our LLPs to jump in so quickly. Even after the boy said "Take easier classes," my brother could have "left the ball" with his son by saying "Then I get the impression you feel good about the way you are progressing in school."

Most people, it seems, have experiences similar to that of my brother. It is a struggle to get started with a new way of responding, and it is difficult to carry through and develop some consistency. We must learn to do what I call "listen again." Listening once to feeling and responding to it is not enough. We might just as well forget about trying to respond to feeling as to do it in the opening response and then forget. Feelings are expressed all of the time, not just in one nice little package that is easy to recognize in the first part of a conversation. Life is daily, communication is daily! We must listen again and again and again for resistance to our acceptance of the feeling to which we addressed ourselves.

If our feeling words are accepted, we may have hit the person's feeling accurately. If the person shows some nonacceptance, then we must try again.

A mother in one of my parent groups asked me, "What comes after we respond to feeling?" My answer was that we still have to choose whether we want to remove ourselves or put ourselves into the life of the speaker. At times we must give the speaker a little of ourselves, but we should consider how often we are doing this. Just how often do our LLPs creep into our responses? If we do not want to make people too dependent on us, then we should continue to respond to feelings and encourage individuals to work out life's difficulties. However, we can mix good responding with some of our LLPs to help people develop on their own while still having a sense of security and a feeling of being loved or accepted. If an individual persists for our solutions or advice, we can say, "I don't know if this will work for you or not, but on occasion it has worked for other people." Or "You will have to decide, but you might consider . . ." is another way to try a suggestion without being too forceful. We cannot allow people to seek our suggestions or advice in such a constant fashion that they become overly dependent on us. I think it best to "keep the ball with them" as long as possible (Gordon, 1970).

Another menacing problem in learning to change our response patterns, especially with "You feel," is the fact that after a while it gets a little corny and does not always come across as real sincere. Of course, we need more than just this one starter to really be able to incorporate a new system into our communication vocabulary.

One class participant told me that her son had done something he was particularly proud of and she said to him, "You feel proud of that," and her son replied, "Mom, where did you get that stuff?" This anecdote illustrates two interesting points: he realized a different type of response and it was a little corny, or at least identifiable. I realize starting with a specific phrase may be a little gimmicky or even disagreeable to some people, but the fact is we just can't start out as experts. We need a conscious point of departure from our old habits. Once the starter response is coming effortlessly to mind, we must strive to develop ways to reflect feeling in a spontaneous and sincere way.

Starters

Below is a list of starters which can be used by all of us, not only to start, but to help us in developing some consistency. We must originate new ways to respond and then practice these new methods enough that they really become a part of our communication system. They should become second nature to us.

Starters
It's as if you . . .
Sounds like you . . .
I get the impression you . . .
I've sort of got the feeling you . . .
It's almost like you . . .
Guess you're saying . . .
You feel as though . . .
Somehow it feels . . .
What you're saying is that you . . .
You are really feeling . . .
So to you it seems like you're feeling . . .
It's like you're (feeling word such as "anxious") . . .
Sounds as though you're really . . .
I am hearing you say that you feel . . .
It seems you . . .

All of these starters will help you begin, but try to respond as you *experience* the feeling someone is trying to send you. I personally don't think it is sound to develop one particular style of responding. A style can get in the way of feeling. I would prefer that a person simply develop a way of listening differently and responding automatically to the feelings heard. You will understand this as you become accomplished and comfortable with yourself in this new communication technique.

Sometimes beginners are at a loss because the feeling being transmitted to us by another is not at first apparent. The "You feel . . ." starter does not lend itself to this situation, but there is an emotion being expressed which needs to be identified. A nonharmful way to respond in such a case, and also a good way to get started, is simply describe back to the person what was said to you. This restatement is the safest thing to say to a person. For example, if your neighbor is really down in the dumps and says to you, "It seems to me the older my kids get, the lazier they get! I do all of the cooking and cleaning. It's a twenty-four-hour job! Why don't they help me out?" How are you going to respond? Obviously, to name a few feeling words, the neighbor sounds disgusted, ignored, demoralized, resentful, and irritated. We may not be clear at first exactly what feeling the neighbor is expressing (the neighbor may not be clear either), but we can respond in a nonthreatening way by *rephrasing* what was said. In this case we might say. "You find yourself doing all of the work since the kid's don't help out much anymore."

The suggested response does not get to the real feeling the neighbor seems to be experiencing, but it allows the person to hear again what he or she said. This is more effective than asking a question, sending one of our grand solutions, or offering some advice arrived at through our illogical use of logic. At least we are not "heaping our stuff" on the person. The response breaks only one of the rules: it does not contain a feeling word.

The rephrasing technique is not the best response, but it can help us get started with a person. It is safe and helps us to overcome many of the obstacles I have mentioned. Many times we become somewhat startled when someone expresses a lot of emotion to us. This rephrasing technique can be helpful in many situations and should be kept on standby. Remember, it is a far better technique than the ones included in our LLP sytem of responding.

Now try taking all of the material you have read so far and begin to apply it in your everyday life. Work to get to the point where it is not thought provoking or a struggle to think about what you are going to say next. This is our major obstacle to overcome, and we must confront it and have courage to keep at it until it becomes a part of us. If the new techniques are applied conscientiously, you should be able to feel your LLPs leaving you. Remember, though, this is just the beginning. There are more obstacles ahead which will be discussed in detail so the reader can formulate a deeper level of understanding as to why some of the rules and suggestions are made in this book and how they can be implemented.

Questions

Several ideas have now been presented and discussed in depth: the setting aside of LLPs, the futility of logic, the importance of responding to feelings and not events, and how to begin with "starter" phrases. This "beginner's kit" should serve the novice well, but there is another rule that must be incorporated here at the outset. This is rule 3 . . . eliminate questions!

The starters suggested will pretty much eliminate the question, but I think it is important for the reader to understand here *why* we must follow this rule to help us in our relationships. Unless it is understood, there may be a temptation to allow questions to creep into our communication. Of course they will always be with us, but we can learn to insert them at a time when they will be most effective.

Many people ask, "How can we find out about a person if we don't ask questions?" When asked this I always insert a personal example. While attending the University of Mississippi, I was involved in many counselor training sessions with Dr. Grady Harlan, Chairman of the Counselor Education Department, and fellow students. During one of the sessions, the class was listening to tapes of counseling sessions recorded by members of the class. During the playing of one of my tapes, Dr. Harlan stopped the tape recorder. He pointed out that I was asking my client many questions. I was challenged to answer when Dr. Harlan asked, "Norm, what are you going to do with all of that stuff?" I thought and really couldn't come up with any good reason as to why I needed to know a lot of "stuff" about this person in order to help him make some adjustment in his life. As a matter of fact, I remember saying to myself that I didn't even have one of my wonderful suggestions for this client, but if I could just dig out a few more facts I would certainly be able to come up with a solution from which we both would benefit. He would use what I suggested to him and I would then feel really good about myself because I would *think* that I had helped this individual overcome his difficulty. Dr. Harlan said, "Why don't you just write out your prescribed program for him?" The point was made very well to all of the class members. Dr. Harlan went on to say that we don't need to collect "stuff" about people that we can punch into a computer in order to help them.

Of course, Dr. Harlan's major point was that we must go with how a person *feels*. We must try to help him understand himself in such a way that he can take action he feels best suits him. The point hit home with me and I hope it does with anyone reading this book.

As I have stated before, research regarding the effectiveness of helpers seems to be tilting toward techniques designed to help a person understand his or her feelings. If we can tune-up our interpersonal communication skills so that we can reflect feeling, or at least let people know their feelings are heard, we will probably be more effective and therefore less harmful to others around us than we are at the present time. Questions do not indicate an awareness of feelings. So the overuse of the question is an obstacle to effective communication.

If we can help people hear themselves as we and others hear them, they may uncover aspects of themselves of which they were not totally aware.[1] (Carkhuff and Berenson, 1967). Now, I ask you, how can any of us help people hear themselves if we choose to only ask questions? When people give out answers, it must be considered that they didn't come up with them on the spur of the moment. The fact that the answers are verbalized is an indication that they were in the people's awareness. They knew the answers well beforehand. If, instead of questioning, we became capable enough to allow them to realize what they are saying in terms of real feelings, they might learn things about themselves they didn't know beforehand and may then act with more understanding about themselves. The question, along with the logic, advice, solutions, assumptions, and responding to an event, takes us too far away from the opportunity to help people hear themselves and clarify their feelings.

Rather than ask a question or use logic, we should ask ourselves,

---

[1] From *Beyond Counseling and Therapy* by Robert Clarkhuff and Bernard G. Berenson. Copyright © 1967 by Holt, Rinehart and Winston, Inc. Reprinted by permission of Holt, Rinehart and Winston, Inc.

"What can we say to this person so that he can hear himself and thereby take something from our talk that will be useful for his development as a person?" (Benjamin, 1969). The ever-popular question that we are discussing nearly always gives the person the impression that we are gathering information about him or her and when we have enough "stuff" we can then send the person a cure for the misery. These individuals learn nothing new about themselves.

I believe the question can be a rather ineffective interpersonal tool, particularly in the beginning stages of a relationship. I also believe we will soon prove that it should be used less than it is now in later stages of most relationships. Too many questions tend to tear down relationships. They too are a misuse of interpersonal power. They seldom allow a person to reflect back on what was just said. A question seeks out new information and does not acknowledge current feeling. It does not acknowledge the fact that you, the listener, are listening very intently.

Use of the question sets us up to break all of the rules. It is often a response to an event, an attempt to reach a logical conclusion, and an ignoring of feeling. The question goes a long way in "stealing the ball from the other person." The individual has to get set to be interrogated. He may want to talk, but, in my opinion, he probably won't; and if he does, he will be saying things that are relatively safe for him. He can answer "Yes," "No," or "I don't know." There is not much feeling given out in these responses.

Somewhere in my background someone pointed out to me that if we, as parents, teachers, counselors, psychologists, or helpers of any kind, ask a lot of questions and then feel good about our helping techniques just because the person is answering most of the time, we could be doing more harm than good. Let's assume we do ask a lot of questions, gather a lot of information, and then tell someone what we think he or she should do. The persons involved have not had the opportunity to rely on their own strengths to conquer their difficulty; they have relied on our strength.

As I mentioned at the beginning of this book, several studies have shown that people who have participated in therapy have become less well adjusted to society than those people who were identified as needing therapy yet did not receive it. Speculation has it that one of the reasons the studies show these discouraging results is that the therapist involved tended to ask too many questions. As a result, many people became reliant on someone else to handle their problems for them. It's true, we are not learning therapy in this book, but many of the same principles apply to interpersonal communication skills. Readers can now begin to understand why we have to try and eliminate as many questions as we can when we are dealing with someone else's feelings. The question simply cheats the person of the chance to grow by relying on his own resources to figure out his next step in life.

Questions far too often *imply* what we think is a possible solution to another person's problems. Let's hypothesize again. Pretend a friend says to you "I am having a rough time making a decision. I have a good job, I like it, but I don't think I'm going to get anywhere unless I go back to school. I don't want to give up the job. God knows I can't afford it yet! I would really like to go to school full time." Some typical responses might be, "Which is more important to you . . . a good job now or in the future?" Or "Why don't you talk to your boss and see what he thinks?" Or "What makes you think you aren't going to get anyplace in your job?" All of these responses are questions and do not reflect feeling. The friend seems to be somewhat discouraged, trapped, stranded, dissatisfied, doubtful, unsure, or puzzled. A better response would be, "Sounds like you are feeling kind of stranded and unsure of what to do." Sure, maybe your friend should talk to the boss; possibly that is the solution. However, if your friend doesn't come up with the idea then whoever gave the idea "took the ball away" and may not be doing the friend a favor. Personally, I believe most people enjoy having their friends bring problems to them because it shows they trust one another. We must be alert in these situations not to ask so many questions and give our friends *our* answers to *their* problems.

Questions, then, are often self-defeating to both people in the communication process. Questions tend to detract from the real purpose of communication, that purpose being to understand each other.

One thing I am absolutely convinced of in the field of the helping professions, is that people who have little or no intention of working on their problems will continue to see a therapist, counselor, psychologist, whomever, as long as the professional asks a lot of questions. These suffering people will therefore not have to take a look at themselves. They will never have feelings reflected back to them. They will answer all of the helper's questions and then the helper will come up with some temporary solution. Each party will go its merry way thinking progress in solving the problem has been made. I think a person can hide true feelings forever if we ask questions forever!

Dr. Alfred Benjamin, an expert in interviewing techniques, has made some excellent observations about the question. He stated that if we ask too many questions the person cannot express himself as openly as he might. He points out that there very often is a very fine line which divides interest *in* a person and curiosity *about* a person. Most people like our interest and not our curiosity. Interest is for the individual's sake and curiosity is for our sake (Benjamin, 1969). I firmly believe that all of us in the helping professions, including teachers and parents, should examine this point closely. People in business might be wise to examine it also. We can eliminate a great amount of threat to effective communication if we try to eliminate curiosity, especially when we are trying to sell a product or help someone work through a difficult situation.

Exploration of the question led Dr. Benjamin to concede that *the question does not need to be eliminated;* it is simply overused. He believes it serves to push a person away from us. He mentions that the word "Why" conveys disapproval or displeasure. He suggested that instead of saying "Why did you fail biology?" we could say "I noticed you failed biology. I'm wondering if I can help?" Or, "I noticed you have been late for work a few times lately, is there some way I could help?" This way we do not lose the respect of a person (Benjamin, 1969).

For the most part "Why" questions are more harmful or less effective than "What" questions. People think they must explain or defend their behavior when asked "Why" and very often this is difficult to do. It is probably better to say "What happened concerning the fight in the hallway?" rather than "Why were you fighting in the hallway?" "What" does not convey as much displeasure, but it is still a question (Benjamin, 1969).

Two authorities in the helping profession, Egan and Benjamin, seem to agree that we should use questions less frequently, leave them open-ended if used, and respond to feeling as soon as we possibly can after we do ask a question.

Interestingly, Egan, in quoting from *The Handbook of Social Psychology* by Deutsch, noted that linking current behavior with a past event is an extremely difficult undertaking (Egan, 1975 p. 105). We must understand that behavior is not usually caused by something which occurred in the past, although questions tend to ask about the past. Current rather than past behavior, is that to which we should address ourselves (Egan, 1975).

We can look at our use of the question in another way. Take time to evaluate what type of responses you get when you ask a question. If you can't use what you get back to arrive at the feeling a person is experiencing, it should begin to tell you something about the questions you are asking (Benjamin, 1969).

Questions are so common in our everyday communication that I fear we will never know how much we overuse them unless we tape record ourselves. I would strongly recommend that readers who work with many people and have to respond to them each day, make arrangements to tape record themselves for several hours and see how many questions they ask and consider just how many were actually needed.

Conversation or Communication?

Enough about logic and questions. There is one other important aspect of communications about which I am compelled to add a brief note in this chapter and that is the difference between a conversation and communication at the feeling level.

There are all kinds of uses for the word "communication." The word means "make known." "Conversation" can be defined as an "informal interchange." We cannot make ourselves known to another person if we only engage in an "informal interchange." If we are trying to understand, and possibly help another individual, it is important to communicate rather than to just engage in conversation. Identifying the difference is a skill we must develop and can only do by practicing.

Learning a new way to relate on a more personal level with people means we must differentiate between when a person is expressing some real feeling and when a person is just engaging in idle chatter. For example, when a husband comes home for dinner and asks his wife "What's for dinner tonight honey?" she should not answer "You sound as though you are curious about what we are having for dinner." This is indeed a real feeling response, but not very good timing. The wife should just answer "Meat loaf." When the communication process takes on a formal nature, we must be alert to pick up the feeling and respond to it. Sometimes there is a very fine line between communication and conversation, but we must teach ourselves to identify it. Remember, we can allow some feeling to pass us by occasionally, but if we miss it very often we can be assured the relationship will begin to degenerate.

In this chapter we have begun with suggested starter phrases to relate to feeling. We have learned to recognize how the use of logic and too many questions can be more harmful than helpful. We should also realize the difference between participating in a conversation and being involved in a serious level of communication. Using these ideas, a comfortable level of the new response pattern is usually realized after several practice sessions, but most people find they must continue to check themselves. The contents of the next chapter should yield even more assistance in making these checks and help us to eliminate our LLPs.

References

Benjamin, Alfred. *The Helping Interview.* Boston: Houghton-Mifflin Co., 1969.

Carkhuff, Robert R. and Berenson, Bernard G. *Beyond Counseling and Therapy.* New York: New York: Holt, Rinehart and Winston, Inc., 1967.

Egan, G. *The Skilled Helper.* Monterey, California: Brooks/Cole Publishing Company, 1975.

Gordon, Thomas. *Parent Effectiveness Training.* Excerpts reprinted with permission from the book *Parent Effectiveness Training* by Gordon. Copyright © 1970. Published by David McKay Co., Inc.

Lillibridge, Michael E. and Klukken, Gary. Interpersonal Communication Skills, Cassette Tape Series, Affective House, Tulsa, Oklahoma, 1977.

Shertzer, B. and Stone, S. *Fundamentals of Guidance.* Boston: Houghton-Mifflin Co., 1976.

Sugarman, Daniel A. *Priceless Gifts.* Copyright © 1978. New York: Macmillian Publishing Company, 1978. Excerpts reprinted by permission of the publisher and Curtis Brown Ltd.

three

More Obstacles

Listening can be looked upon as the beginning of understanding. It is a sign of respect; it can erase some anxiety and offers hope to those having difficulty. Although it seems to be the most disregarded, it is probably the most important factor in human communication. If this is true, and I believe it is, we should now be realizing that in order to change our typical form of communication, we must learn to listen and hear *differently.* We can learn to respond better only if we hear things better. It should be very clear to the reader by now that just because we heard every word someone said doesn't necessarily mean we heard his true feelings. Picking up feeling requires listening. Hearing is not the same as listening! Being a good hearer is not the same as being a good listener!

There are several factors that can assist us in understanding the vital differences between hearing and listening. We can become better listeners if we just become aware of these factors and check ourselves out occasionally to make sure we are applying them.

One such factor to consider is that we can listen faster than we can talk. Think about that for a minute! Think about all the ideas that may run through our heads when someone is talking with us. We can listen and then conjure up many thoughts before we make a response. There is, then, *time on our side,* time we can use to better understand what a person is "feeling" as well as what he is saying. In a sense we are going in behind the words. As apprentices in changing our communication techniques, we can use this time to our advantage.

First, we must understand that this "extra" time is usually spent to organize a question or to arrive at some miraculous solution or magical advice. Since we eliminated those not-so-magical responses in the last chapter, we now have a time void in which we can insert something more meaningful than we are normally accustomed to doing. It is within this period of "extra" time that we could make an effort to listen for feeling, forget the event or situation a good percentage of the time, and apply a good feeling word to our next response. It is within this gap in time, I firmly believe, that the mysterious "generation gap" has slowly been created by us. Allow me to explain!

Generation Gap

The term "generation gap" obviously was originated by someone who noted that adults and teenagers or parents and children really don't seem to understand each other. My contention is that this gap is none other than the one I just described. The gap has been constantly filled with violations of the seven rules we learned earlier. We erroneously use the gap to send solutions, ask questions, give advice, misuse logic, or conjure up other ways to break the rules. We are so involved in our own responses, that we are oblivious to the idea that someone's feelings are involved other than our own, and our responses start the relationship reeling. The gap, improperly used, is the exact point where misunderstandings occur. It is the time the spirit of another person is diminished because his expressions are not received (Moustakas, 1975).

I do, however, find it unfair to apply the term "generation gap" specifically to teenage and adult differences. We might just as well call it the "divorce gap" or the "employer/employee gap" or the "family gap" or the "marriage gap." It is difficult for me to comprehend why we use the term "generation gap" when the "gap," improperly used, causes just as many problems between people of similar ages. It seems to me we are saying adults get along better with each other than with kids. Whom are we kidding? With all of the marriage and personal problems we see in this country, it really seems a shame we have not coined a nice little phrase to apply to the large group of people who experience these problems. The gap is present in all relationships at all ages.

The Relationship Gap

With this larger application in mind, I prefer the term "relationship gap" and I define it as: *That improperly used period of time which lies between that instant someone begins to say something to us and the instant we start to respond.* It is at this exact gap time that our thoughts should refer us to our rules, our feeling word list, and our starters to help us regenerate the spirit. By using this time efficiently, we can fill the gap with better responses, which we have sorrowfully been lacking.

Another way to avoid using the gap improperly is to conscientiously check ourselves to see if we miss the feeling a person sends us. If we break the rules too often and miss picking up feeling, an alienation develops. According to Dr. Moustakas, "Self-confidence is reduced by failure to be heard and new avenues of gaining recognition are sought. Attention-getting methods are invoked that do not represent real interests, attitudes, perceptions, or talents" (Moustakas, 1975, p. 1). Soon it becomes more difficult to clean up the remnants of not being heard than it does to clean up the remnants of an oil slick. The only way we can eliminate the alienation is to fill the relationship gap with something better. The gap can and should be something good.

All people, to some extent are in the relationship gap and it has flourished for years. One researcher recently wrote that parents and their offspring quarrel about the same amount and mostly about the same subjects as they did in 1924![1] Words and our use of them have not changed much in fifty years. Isn't it clear that misunderstandings, inability to respond to feeling, and lack of skill in settling disagreements constructively are the constant variables when we attempt to discover why relationships suffer?

Each individual in our society has, or soon will have, created

---

[1] Reprinted by permission from *TIME, The Weekly Newsmagazine;* Copyright © *Time, Inc.,* 1978. (Excerpt from "Middletown Revisited.")

his or her own width in the gap by the way he or she listens and responds. He controls his gap by what he thinks about or hopefully experiences from what the other person reveals about himself. In adult relationships each person must be responsible to "fill in the gap." In child-adult relationships, the burden for now is with the adult. We do at this point have within our grasp material that can help us fill in the gap, but listening at a deep level and hearing feeling is in many respects a prerequisite to using the rules and other suggestions. Proper listening and responding can allow the positive narrowing of the gap. The gap is controllable!

Many parents have asked me, "Where do the kids come into all of this?" I always answer by saying that of course kids should also be taught these skills. Ideally, we should teach listening and responding skills in our schools if for no other reason than that schools are where we learn to formulate relationships. Along with homes, schools develop personalities that soon encounter other personalities. Since children are capable of learning these same communication skills, we should be able to eliminate the gap and humanize our schools and homes.

However, we need a starting point and schools thus far haven't taken the lead. We don't know which came first . . . the chicken or the egg. However, we do know that parents come before kids. I, therefore, think the burden is primarily on parents and teachers and other adults to try to eliminate any alienation and attempt to build good relationships.

Young people will be more likely to participate in the relationships and trust adults if we fill the relationship gap with words that foster independence, trust, and good emotional growth.

We can fill this gap with such positive responses by using the suggestions and rules presented in the previous chapters if we first become good listeners. Some people become frightened at such a prospect. That is, they are very aware they have time to listen and respond better, but they have not practiced putting the rules, word list, and starters *in the gap* enough to feel comfortable in the new process. Often because they find it difficult to respond, they remain silent. This silence is caused because it seems somewhat easier to hear feeling than it is to respond to feeling. They think, and rightfully so, that what they have been saying has been more harmful than what they previously thought and they believe it is safer to remain quiet. It isn't! To avoid being harmful by being silent is to replace one obstacle with another. The object of learning to listen deeper is to be able to respond to feelings better. Being quiet is not the answer! We must participate in the communication process. It could be dangerous not to take part. Many people see it as being dangerous to participate, but it seems a great majority of these people are insecure and are afraid of what they might learn. If we remain quiet, though, people might get the impression that we are bored with what they shared with us, or perhaps worse, that we don't understand what we heard in the way of feeling, or that we just don't care. Being quiet will not close the gap.

There is also the chance that when we do become fairly comfortable with the new responding process, we might begin casting our "stuff" into the gap. To eliminate that pitfall, consider this resolution as a possibility: "I no longer include in my vocabulary the statement, 'I know how you feel.' It is not part of me anymore." I just don't think we really know how someone else feels. We may have some idea, such as when a loved one dies, but even then we can't be sure someone close to us feels the same way we do. Your headache may feel different than mine. Your disappointment may feel different than my disappointment. Your discouragement or excitement may be more intense than mine.

Listening

I think it is safer and a better way to become a good listener for feeling if we just tell ourselves that we can't tell how someone feels because of an *event* he has chosen to describe to us. We can hope to communicate with him by trying to hit the proper feeling level when we respond, but we cannot assume we have felt the same way he has just because we have experienced a similar event in our lives. Feelings are very complex and just because we *think* "we have been there" isn't quite enough evidence about feeling to apply it to another person's situation. We should try and make sure it is that person's feeling we are responding to and not our feeling.

Furthermore, our listening skills can be refined to a point where the other person knows he is being heard and will not have to use his energy to think up some system to avoid spilling out his feelings to us. We can be relatively sure we have listened well if, after a response by us, the person continues to discuss his feelings. It is my experience that people who know we are truly listening and are genuinely interested in them will often correct us if we happen to miss their feeling. They will either give us the proper feeling word or give us a hint we should search for a better one. For example, if we say "You seem somewhat discouraged," and someone says "Well, slightly, but I'm not giving up, I just won't quit," then it is best to switch to the current expressed feeling and say something like "Your confidence is still high and you think you can make it." This is slightly better than saying "You aren't so discouraged anymore." We should, in most cases, go with the feeling just heard and not that from the past. Most people improve attitudes and behaviors when they know they are listened to and are not in the presence of someone who is just collecting information so he can apply his or her magical solutions.

Another personal example of my own might be helpful in conquering the obstacles associated with listening. A boy I was counseling with was very upset about the fact that his parents had just told him they were getting a divorce. He said, "In the upcoming settlement my Mom is getting a thousand dollars a month and my Dad is *only* getting seven hundred." My response was, "You seem to be concerned about your Dad getting fair treatment." He surprised me when he said, "No, not really, not after what he did to Mom." Possibly I clarified his feelings for him and he didn't think he should be feeling that way, or he didn't say what he was really feeling, or possibly, I just missed it and he gave me a clue as to how he really did feel about his Dad *only* getting seven hundred dollars. I will never know for sure just how he felt. I was merely trying to make sure he was heard by someone interested in him. I have never been directly involved in a divorce and even if I had, I am sure I wouldn't have "felt" the same way he did.

In concentrating on listening and the factors involved with it, we must create within ourselves a very sincere desire to hear another person. However, once we do begin to better hear and therefore understand another person's feelings, we will no doubt have to go through another change similar to the one we encountered in the first two chapters when we learned about how to respond differently.

Dr. Thomas Gordon, author of *Parent Effectiveness Training,* pointed out that we run the risk of having our opinions and attitudes change when we become better listeners (Gordon, 1970). I believe changes must take place in people if they are to have any chance of incorporating these skills into their communication systems. It is almost a necessity. Furthermore, we must develop an attitude that we will hear a great deal from others with which we don't agree, but we just cannot allow ourselves to get in the way again. Indeed this "wanting to disagree" is an obstacle to overcome, but the seven rules conscientiously applied will help us overcome the desire to disagree with a person we are trying to help work through some life difficulty.

Another factor I think we should consider is that we cannot listen while we are talking or getting ready to talk. Often no real listening takes place because people simply take turns talking. We must try to experience what the other person is saying in the way of feeling and we can't if we are so excited about what we are going to say next. It seems we sometimes fill the gap with pet remarks without "listening again" for the possibility of any feeling being expressed. Some "pet remarks" I hear rather frequently are listed here just to acquaint the reader with a few of them:

> Don't worry about it.
> You'll get over it in time.
> It will all work out in the end.
> Take the good with the bad.
> Time will take care of it.
> There is no reason to be afraid.
> Worrying won't do any good.
> That's not so bad, happens all the time.

When we make remarks like this and real feeling is involved it is almost like we are saying to a person, "Keep talking, I'll check in every so often." This is the exact time we miss a person's feeling.

We can develop the attitude of becoming excited about "hearing someone's feelings" rather than channeling our excitement into what we are about to say. We usually say something because the desire to do so evolves from two "socially mandated" habits. First, we erroneously believe that we can impress others by talking and, secondly, we spend most of our time thinking about ourselves and, as a result, we usually respond with ourselves in mind.

We don't have to talk to impress others. We can leave a far better impression by the way we listen. Consider the following example of listening and leaving a good impression. Friends of mine, a family of six, visited Europe recently. While having dinner in a German restaurant, they were impressed by a waiter who asked for each individual order and never wrote anything down; yet he delivered every item in the large order. The waiter had trained himself to listen and think about other people. Yes, we can leave a far better impression by the way we listen!

We seem to manage other parts of our bodies and even our emotions better than our mouths. It is for this reason that I think many people seeking help for some problem they are encountering will run a little test during the first session with the "helper." They will engage in idle chatter, but throw out some feeling during the course of the conversation just to see if the helper is listening for it. If the feeling isn't picked up these people will go to someone else for help. Many people in the helping professions, as well as in the business world, lose clients because they fail this little test. I'm sure all people use this technique in establishing relationships even if it is subconscious in nature. This is just one reason why so many people do not return a second time to a helper, continue with a businessperson, or seek to further develop a relationship with someone.

In the helping professions we often hear "He just didn't want to get any better." This is often the case, but not as often as we may now assume. The person suffering some life difficulty may be saying "He is really not interested in me," or "He wasn't listening to me." The helper may have been interested (most are), but his listening and responding techniques didn't convey that attitude. We must understand that it is very human to want to be heard and sometimes just being heard is enough!

While we are on the subject of listening, I hope we can lay to rest the old saying "Kids should be seen and not heard." I realize this phrase was originated to let kids know they should not interrupt or be noisy when someone else is talking. Neither should adults for that matter. We tend to carry the "not heard" part too far by the way we listen. If the kids aren't heard, they may not be seen . . . they may run away as thousands do every year!

Although there are many variables present when trying to measure the effect of one person upon another, I think one rather reliable measure of effectiveness in listening is when a person says to you "Thanks for the advice," and you didn't give any! This simply means that you were very skillful in helping that individual explore his feelings and come up with a decision that is comfortable for him. It is the ideal ending of a helping situation.

There are many reasons why we seldom approach the perfect results regarding listening and responding. I have attempted to categorize some of the obstacles that I have observed as ingrained LLPs in the majority of us and which prevent us from listening and responding more effectively. These are things we *usually* say or do almost everyday that hinder us from filling the "relationship gap" with proper responses. Of course, proper responses in turn come from effective listening. We fall into these traps to escape having to consider someone's feelings. Perhaps it will help the reader to see how our LLPs have been surfacing during the gap time by examining some of these categories.

Advicers, Solutioners, and Suggestioners

First, let's look at the *Advicers, Solutioners,* and *Suggestioners.* Many of us could be labeled as such because we have the ingrained need to break the rule against giving advice. When we spend a great deal of our response time sending these types of messages, it seems as though we do fit under these labels. It's as if we know more about the person than he knows about himself.

These empty responses to feeling indicate to a person that we don't really have much confidence in his ability to work out a solution to his own problems. This habit of giving advice is not a healthy one in establishing relationships. If we are in this category, we unconsciously transfer the idea that we are the superior person. Far too often, when we become advicers, solutioners, or suggestioners we send the message that we didn't hear the person or that we don't quite believe him. It doesn't matter what he says; our advice is preplanned. The teacher who says "You need to study more," fits into this category.

Here is another good example of an advicer or suggestioner or solutioner at work. A girl says to her father "I could have done better with my grades, but Mrs. Lackofeeling is a real jerk." The father joins the category when he sends back that seemingly All-American response, "You will meet people all through your life whom you won't like. Sometimes you just have to adjust to them." This is advice to the nth degree and in no way assists the girl to examine her feelings.

A better response might be "It's like you could have accomplished more, but you are dissatisfied with one teacher." Responses of this type remove the dependency people have for advice.

Possibly we feel better about ourselves if we have a lot of people depending on us. If this is true we must keep in mind that dependency is one of our great social problems. People depending too much on other people is one of our current unrecognized social problems. I firmly believe that "irresponsible responders" such as those of us being described here, help breed more drug addicts, people with emotional problems, and, yes, even alcoholics, than any causative factor we can currently identify. These people are dependent and escape to what is to them a more comfortable existence. They have never learned to depend on their own strengths for making adjustments in their lives.

Advicers, solutioners, and suggestioners serve to develop dependent people. Dependent people are too reliant on other people to make decisions for them. I have learned that inability to make decisions is a symptom of mental illness. So we can see the importance of removing dependency in our communication systems.

Consider the thought that we may subconsciously become advicers, solutioners, or suggestioners because we do hear a great amount of feeling and we then become anxious in our inability to handle it comfortably. We then send advice or a quick solution in hopes the problem will go away. We seem to respond in such a way that we are more concerned with our comfort level than that of the person with whom we are talking. We may already be comfortable and just aren't willing to give up any of our comfort, or, we may be genuinely concerned for the other person's comfort, and erroneously think that our solution will take away their problems.

Judgers, Analyzers, Evaluators, and Concluders

This brings us to the second category of rule offenders: *Judgers, Analyzers, Evaluators,* and *Concluders.* When we find ourselves in this group, we are usually saying to a person's expressed feelings that we have finally figured out what is wrong with him, and we can now give him a magnificent plan for his self-improvement. Out comes our self-proclaimed magical power again! The problem with being an evaluator, judger, analyzer, or concluder is this: If we *are* accurate in our evaluations (usually we aren't), the person may be embarrassed; if we are wrong, the person may very well become angry with us for judging him erroneously.

An example of this category is described here: A teenage boy says to his counselor, "Please promise not to tell anyone, but I have to talk to someone about the CB I stole last week. It is getting to me." There are those counselors or parents or other adults who might say, "I guess you are feeling bad because you know stealing is not acceptable in our society." The counselor, parent, teacher, whomever, has "judged" the behavior to be bad. He has analyzed and evaluated the behavior and concluded that in order for him to help this young man, he must once again remind him that stealing is not acceptable in our society. How can that be helpful? Right, it can't! It seems we often think that if we can just get the person to feel truly guilty and hang his head in shame that we are successful in our attempts to help him (Benjamin, 1969). This only serves to embarrass the individual if he does feel guilty. If the person does not feel guilty and the counselor or parent is wrong, then the individual could become upset and strike back. At any rate, we can't win when we find ourselves in this category. Judging, evaluating, analyzing, and concluding mixed with poor use of logic can cause chaos in a counseling session or in a "relationship session."

We must understand that judging, evaluating, and analyzing do not work even if we do come close to hitting the real feeling. If we judge feelings people will quickly learn to keep their feelings away from us to avoid being hurt or having to become angry. It is safer to simply use a starter such as "I get the impression you are feeling somewhat guilty and want to ventilate your feelings a little bit."

I am convinced our overwhelming need to be a judger is, in part, to blame for our problems in schools, families, and in business. It seems to me when we have already judged or analyzed someone's behavior to be uncooperative or antagonistic to us or simply irresponsible or eccentric, that we continue to believe by the way we respond to him that he will continue this behavior. No one around this person, virtually no one, tries to pick up any feeling from him. He receives very little in the way of human nourishment.[2] He will stay the way

<hr>

[2] From *BEYOND COUNSELING AND THERAPY* by Robert R. Carkhuff and Bernard G. Berenson. Copyright (c) 1967 by Holt, Rinehart and Winston, Inc. Reprinted by permission of Holt, Rinehart and Winston.

he is because he is not afforded the opportunity to be otherwise by someone skillful enough to help him take a look at his behavior. He is not allowed to look at a way out of his dilemma! Even if our conclusions or judgments are right, what have we spent of ourselves if we instead, just try to apply our rules and help the person recognize his feelings?

There is little doubt that our values do influence what we say and I'm not advocating that we disregard these values. We can't just cast aside the things we believe in, but I think we must be aware that judging and jumping to conclusions about someone's problems or ideas seldom leads to pleasant conclusions. As most of the other obstacles to good communications mentioned in this book, we just use them all far too often. We fill the gap with our "stuff" without being aware what damage it really can do.

Minimizers

In our next category, *Minimizers,* we can see examples galore everyday. So many, in fact, that I have chosen to place it in a category by itself.

"Don't worry about it," ranks very high on the all-time hit parade as a minimizer response. We should be careful using this response when someone seems really concerned about something, for we are then relaying to him that what he is telling us is not really as important as he is attempting to tell us it is.

We place ourselves in the minimizer category when we fail to come close to responding to pleasant or unpleasant feelings. We may not actually hear feeling or we don't want to take the time to reflect it back to a person. As a result we become a minimizer.

Another example of a minimizer is a father who asks his son how he did in the baseball game. His son says, "I got two hits and drove in the winning run." The father becomes a minimizer when he says, "Good! I'll bet you are choking up on the bat more just like I told you to do." Or, even worse, an overly anxious father might say, "That's great! Did you have any errors today?," which just adds more of himself than is needed. It is almost like the people that respond in this manner are looking for imperfections in others so they can feel better about themselves. Just allow the youngster to enjoy his good day!

If someone says "I've got a paper due for my course in just three days," and we respond "Keep at it, things will work out," it sounds good and isn't bad some of the time, but it doesn't do much to help the person look at his problem. A better response might be "Sounds like you're pressed a little."

"I just went over that material ten minutes ago," is a minimizing response by a teacher. It may hinder the interaction the teacher is trying to promote in his or her class. Paying attention to little exchanges such as these is more important than we might think when we consider the effect of them over a long period of time in our relationships.

Of course, when we become a minimizer we run the risk of conveying to people that we didn't hear their feelings. Soon they may say to themselves that there is little reason to discuss with us how they feel about things. No single minimizing response wrecks a marriage, a classroom, a business, or a relationship, but added together over a long period of time, they can become devastating. Like water dripping on a rock, a feelingless response tends to penetrate deeper the longer it drips (Gordon, 1970). Our only hope is that people will spend half as much time learning these new responses as they have spent injecting ineffective ones into people around them.

Persuaders

Persuaders are easily identifiable in our society. When the mother tells her daughter, who is being left out of a group, to "try and be nicer," she has become a persuader. When we catch ourselves begging or pleading to someone to change behavior, we are in this category. It seldom is effective! We must be aware that merely letting a person know the facts the way *we* see them does not change his feelings about an event in his life. "Don't let them get to you," is an attempt by use of logic to persuade the bad feelings out of a person. It is amazing how much difficulty we have in getting rid of our own bad feelings, when we seem to think it is relatively simple to become a persuader and relieve stress in someone else. It is almost like saying to ourselves, "If I don't think this problem is so bad, the other person won't either."

Often, when we become a persuader, we are telling an individual he is wrong in his method of working out the problem. We so much have the need to be right that it is difficult for us not to become a persuader. When we persuade and persuade, it is like saying to a person "You become more like me and everything will be O.K." In my view, we spend far too much time trying to persuade people that they should feel differently. We can teach ourselves to influence people rather than coerce them. Here again, if we persuade people to use our magical solutions we are depriving those people of a chance to be independent . . . and most people enjoy and need their independence!

I think we often mistake persuasion for encouragement. Persuasion comes across as *"You should do this"* whereas encouragement comes across as *"You might try this."* People will more likely make a good decision when given a choice. This type of encouragement works best when the person we are talking with indirectly mentions a solution which is something similar to that which we have in mind. If a suggestion is accepted, it comes off as just a suggestion and not heavy persuasion.

As I mentioned before, some of the rules *must* be broken occasionally, and now we see it is necessary since we know we must make suggestions, give advice, and even persuade in some situations. It is simply a matter of good judgment as to when we choose to place ourselves in the categories mentioned here. Keep in mind that the rules should not be absolutes to adhere to rigidly, nor should it be standard procedure for us to avoid these categories like the plague. It is, though, beneficial to live by the rules and stay out of these categories much more often than we normally do.

We can see some of the complexity involved with human communication and interaction when we become more experienced in understanding how encouragement can easily turn into persuasion. For example, if we hear someone say "Sounds like a good idea," he or she may be accepting our advice and we are not into the persuasion game. However, if a person says "Sound like a good idea, but . . . ," this "but" should be a clue that the person doesn't *really* think it is such a good idea. The individual is looking for some alterations. "Yes, but" or "what if" are other word clues that our persuasion is not working for us (Lillibridge, 1977). Clues of this type can help us become more sensitive to a person and more careful not to carry our persuasion or advice too far. I think we overlook these clues because we want people to accept our logic, solutions, advice, or suggestions.

At any rate, I hope I have persuaded you . . . whoops!, encouraged you to refrain from becoming as much of a persuader as you have probably been in the past.

Moralizers

Those of us who seem to belong in the *Moralizer* category may have learned an LLP that is very difficult to eradicate. By our comments we suggest to people that they should feel guilty about their feelings. In addition to coming across as neglecting all feelings, we convey a lack of trust. To my mind, this is one of the most common forms of saying "I can shape you up," but is, in fact, one of the worst rule breakers and helps to put people down.

Let's consider an example of a moralizer. A young adult is caught shoplifting and the parents are informed of the illegal activity. The youngster feels bad and doesn't know what to expect from his parents. The parents become moralizers instead of helpers when they say "You know it is not right to steal. We have been over that before. You have to think before you act. If this incident goes on your record, it could follow you the rest of your life. You have to think more of yourself." It is very difficult not to moralize in a case such as this, especially when someone is so close to us. We want to implant our value system *now!* As you might suspect, I do not think this form of impatience and moralizing does much to help the youngster. It can and does cause many relationships to suffer.

In his book on helping, Benjamin suggested a better response to protect against becoming a moralizer. He suggested the following when a moral issue is at stake: The young shoplifter will not be hurt as much if the parents respond with "It's as if it is wrong, but you did it (or continue to do it) and are not sure why" (Benjamin, 1969). This comes close to affording the youngster an opportunity to look at himself. Somehow it does seem better than a common moralizer response such as "You know it isn't right to take something that belongs to someone else." Yes, I know we must teach values and morals, but constant moralizing may defeat the purpose. It may become demoralizing!

Questioners, Probers, and Investigators

Questioning, with its damaging effects on a relationship, was explored extensively in Chapter II, so I will not dwell on it here. However, I think it is important to emphasize again how ineffective it is to fill the relationship gap with statements designed to probe or investigate someone. So allow me to introduce the *Questioners, Probers,* and *Investigators.*

Appropriate questioning to get at feeling is needed; probing questions intended to collect meaningless information are not. We often ask inappropriate questions because we erroneously believe people won't talk unless they are asked questions. (See Chapter II about "questions".)

I reiterate that it is ineffective to gather facts about people in order to help them decide where they want to go with their lives. The facts may be important for them to look at, but not as a result of us picking and then choosing which facts are the most important for them to consider. If we show we can listen and respond to feelings, we are then and only then, showing our concern about where people are going. Also, those of us who are parents may not be so disappointed when the kids end up somewhere that we didn't exactly have in mind for them.

Anticipators, Assumptionists, and Interveners

The final category is that of the *Anticipators, Assumptionists,* and *Interveners.* We give ourselves away as noncaring people more quickly in this group than in any of the other groups mentioned in this chapter. We don't even give the gap a chance to form before we thrust ourselves on someone. We fill in the gap before it is opened.

Benjamin related to the idea that our need to talk, unfortunately, is often greater than our ability to listen (Benjamin, 1969). I think we can label ourselves as anticipators, assumptionists, or interveners when we start talking and breaking the rules before the other person even finishes a sentence. All we seem to need is just a few clues about the problem and we impose our personal advice on the speaker. Often we serve only to distort reality and increase anxiety levels of those around us.

Carkhuff and Berenson in their book entitled *Beyond Counseling and Therapy*, suggested we check ourselves to make sure we are "with a person" rather than "beyond a person" [3] (Carkhuff and Berenson, 1967 p. 136). We are beyond someone when we assume the role of an anticipator, assumptionist, or intervener. A couple of examples I have observed are included here in order to help the reader better understand the concept of being "beyond" a person in the communication process.

One evening my wife and I were having dinner with several couples, one of whom had lived in Europe, and the conversation turned to foreign travel. Someone asked, "What are the golf courses like in Europe?" The lady who had lived in Europe answered, "You don't go to Europe to play golf." She was, with that response, "beyond" the person asking the question. She became an assumptionist. She "assumed" or had some preconceived idea that people should go to Europe for reasons *other* than the one being inquired about. As a result of her assumption, an answer was not pursued and she stifled the conversation with the inclusion of this obstacle. This is a classic example of a very common conversation turning into a poor "relationship session." The relationship gap was not filled with the proper words. When we assume or anticipate too much about a person, we don't show respect for his individuality; we are "beyond" his thoughts and feelings.

Another example of "being beyond" centers around a tragic death which occurred in my community. A young boy, a first-year high school student, was electrocuted after he climbed a tree and came in contact with electrical power lines. Following this incident, the father called the power company inquiring about ways to prevent such a catastrophe from happening again. During the course of the father's conversation with the representative of the power company,

---

[3] From *BEYOND COUNSELING AND THERAPY* by Robert R. Carkhuff and Bernard G. Berenson. Copyright © 1967 by Holt, Rinehart and Winston, Inc. Reprinted by permission of Holt, Rinehart and Winston.

the representative said, "What was the boy doing up in the tree anyway?" The representative was "beyond," far beyond, the father's attempt to deal with his feelings and be listened to. I have to ask "Don't boys climb trees?" and even this seems irrelevant to the father's feelings and his question of what can be done.

This is just another example of an individual assuming too much, using logic, asking a poor question, responding to an event instead of someone's feelings, and generally failing to relate at a very effective level. The representative was so far "beyond" the father that he only served to deteriorate the communication process and most certainly failed to bolster the public image of his company!

We, as anticipators, assumptionists, and interveners give ourselves away when we "take the ball" from the other person by blocking the flow of words that we could use to identify feeling or communicate understanding. We show a lack of concern and interest when we place ourselves in this category. As soon as people can label us as an anticipator, assumptionist, or intervener, we can rest assured they won't be around much to share their world with us.

It is rare to find someone who has the ability to listen and then not be coiled as if ready to spring on us with God-sent solutions. People in this group tend to arrive at this "ready-to-pounce" action rather quickly and, of course, this is preceded by not listening thoroughly. As we now know, we do have the time to listen and think, but as this category suggests, we simply don't use the time properly.

As anticipators, we simply anticipate what a person is going to say or we become assumptionists when we assume we know what is coming next from a person's mouth. We think we have more than likely heard it before and aren't too anxious to listen to it again. Often this type of responder uses the gap time to erroneously anticipate or assume, but then fails to recognize that he is wrong and makes some harmful response. *"We hear what we want to hear"* may be a very profound statement for people in our society to consider. Doesn't it seem that we often listen just long enough to hear what *we expect* the person to say? It certainly applies in the case of anticipators, assumptionists, and interveners.

We include the use of many of these obstacles in our everyday lives, I believe, because they allow us to feel powerful. When we feel powerful, we think we feel better or *are* better than someone else. I maintain this is an illusion. We can feel better about ourselves on a more permanent basis if we can eliminate these obstacles.

When we try to help someone, or are just trying to establish a relationship, and still have these obstacles "ingrained" within us, we are grasping to our LLPs and are participating in what is commonly called "one-up-manship."

We should consider the fact that while we are trying to help or establish rapport with someone, many people do not want to improve themselves or at least don't see how they can. It follows that people trying to help them, but who still subscribe to the obstacles just described, will receive a great deal of good feedback and good recommendations as a helper because they unknowingly allow a person to wallow in his misery. The person doesn't have to make any changes in his behavior and often that is very comfortable for him.

Intimidate or Melba Milquetoast?

A person must feel comfortable with, rather than intimidated by, another person before he will reveal himself. The obstacles mentioned in this chapter often prevent us from creating a comfortable level with another person. Most of the categories mentioned tend to intimidate other people. Strong advice and suggestions, constant judging and persuading, along with moralizing and probing can be called fringe intimidation. This fringe intimidation is designed for our own purposes and not for the real benefit of anyone else.

We can be assertive, but keep in mind we can only guide growth; we can't force it (Sugarman, 1978). Much has been written about being assertive, but I'm afraid too much has been misunderstood. Many people seem to confuse assertiveness with intimidation. It is my view that we should attempt to find a "mild in-between" or a balance, in order to eliminate this confusion. We don't have to become Melba Milquetoast nor should we come on as the judge and jury. We do tend to come on in this intimidating way when we constantly place ourselves in the categories just described. Intimidation threatens our egos and friction often develops when peace of mind is disturbed. Our LLPs, unbeknownst to us, often promote this friction.

Obviously, I am suggesting that we consider how often these

obstacles rob us of an opportunity to apply a sensitive touch to some-one's feelings. It is often difficult to help parents, teachers, counselors, nurses, people in business, and so on, to realize the full value of understanding the obstacles. Of course, I believe that when people become thoroughly familiar with these rules, starters, feeling word list, and obstacles they can relate to people on a much better level. It is easy for those trained in these skills to identify those who are clinging to their LLPs. I think we can now say, at this point in the book, that clinging to LLPs means breaking the rules too often and not recognizing what obstacles we need to overcome.

See the Light

Recently, while teaching a graduate class in counseling techniques, I discovered that one of my students was not making the progress of learning these skills as well as the other students. After several sessions of explaining the communication techniques discussed in this book, the student said, "After we learn all of these techniques, how do we make the kids see the light?" Another student spoke up and said, "We first have to understand that their light may be different than our light." The reaction of the class, by facial and verbal clues, clearly demonstrated their agreement with the last student and indicated to me their understanding of the correlation of LLPs to the obstacles.

To change our LLPs, to experience some stress, to take some time and risk, is difficult and not often attempted, particularly by adults. A would-be helper who breaks all of the rules and clings to the obstacles just described, can carry on, but will seldom be effective in bringing about constructive change. The sad thing is that these would-be helpers can feel very good about themselves and many un-helped persons will tell these "helpers" that they should feel good about all the wonderful assistance they are giving people. People attempting to help other people should be realistic and if they do not have evidence that the behavior has changed, they shouldn't dupe themselves into thinking they were effective in changing behavior. "Catch 22" was nothing like this dilemma going on in our homes, schools, churches, businesses, counseling agencies, hospitals, and hot lines.

BENJAMIN, ALFRED. *The Helping Interview.* Boston: Houghton-Mifflin Co., 1969.

CARKHUFF, ROBERT R. and BERENSON, BERNARD G. *Beyond Counseling and Therapy.* New York: Holt, Rinehart and Winston, Inc., 1967.

GORDON, THOMAS. *Parent Effectiveness Training.* (c) 1970. Reprinted with permission from the book *Parent Effectiveness Training* by Gordon. Copyright (c) 1970. Published by David McKay Co., Inc.

LILLIBRIDGE, MICHAEL E. and KLUKKEN, GARY. Interpersonal Communication Skills, Cassette Tape Series, Affective House, Tulsa, Oklahoma, 1977.

MOUSTAKAS, G. *Who Will Listen?* New York: Ballantine Books (A Division of Random House), 1975.

SUGARMAN, DANIEL A. *Priceless Gifts.* Copyright (c) 1978. New York: Macmillian Publishing Company, 1978.

TIME, The Weekly Magazine. Reprinted by permission from *TIME, The Weekly Newsmagazine;* Copyright (c) *Time, Inc.,* 1978. (Excerpt from article "Middletown Revisited," October. 1976.)

four

The Final Effect of LLPs

As a youngster I heard Gene Autry and other singers sing a song entitled "Home On the Range." In this song was a line which always intrigued me, but, at such a young age, the meaning of the words had little impact on me. Now they do! The line was: Home, home on the range, where seldom is heard a discouraging word, and the skies are not cloudy all day. The line implies that "home on the range" is a nice place to be, that people there *encourage* each other, that conflicts between people are few and far between, that verbal muggings rarely occur.

The phrase "where seldom is heard a discouraging word" seems appropriate to use to introduce this chapter. The chapter will discuss the *final* effects of our LLPs and possibly more important, attempt to explain how people who cling to their LLPs and allow themselves to consistently place themselves in the categories mentioned in the last chapter actually affect people around them. Very simply, these people *discourage* the people around them. Those discouraged people are family members, employees, students, patients, or whomever.

Dr. Lewis Losoncy, in his well-thought-out book, *Turning People On—How to Be an Encouraging Person*, mentions that "we live in a world in which we are all more able to discourage than encourage" (Losoncy,

1977 p. x). Of course the material presented in this book is intended to teach the concept that our LLPs might have something to do with kids running away, becoming drug addicts, alcoholics, prostitutes, dropouts, thieves, and suicide victims. They have grown up in a discouraging atmosphere (Losoncy, 1977).

The real effect of our costly LLPs is discouragement. As we have learned, this process of using our LLPs to bring about discouragement is an unintentional, very subtle process. The results we don't want, but often can't seem to avoid.

We have looked at some ideas in communication in the first three chapters that have tremendous effect on our relationships. There are *still* other obstacles in personal communication we must overcome if we are to improve the quality of our relationships. There are still "discouraging words" spoken in our society that should "seldom be heard."

The Praise/Criticism Dilemma

A dilemma in personal communication, which we might call the praise/criticism dilemma, produces many problems in our attempts to eliminate our LLPs and become more encouraging people. The father who said, "Keep up the good work, grades are important," and then when the grades headed downward said, "Aren't you working? Your grades are going down," was participating in the praise/criticism dilemma. Most of us, like the father, cannot leave our LLPs out and make an encouraging remark *regardless* of the seemingly discouraging event taking place in our lives. We must, it seems, either praise or criticize, yet this praise/criticism dilemma often creates the discouraging atmosphere we want to avoid.

We could benefit from becoming more able to recognize when we are headed for this dilemma and developing methods to counteract it. Our seven rules, listed here for review, if applied properly, can prevent the possibility of our getting involved in the praise/criticism dilemma. The rules prevent us from participating in the "discouraging atmosphere" (Losoncy, 1977).

1. Take the feeling, not the event.
2. Use a feeling word. Don't minimize feelings.

3. Eliminate questions!
4. Eliminate logic and assumptions.
5. Don't send solutions or give advice.
6. Allow them to do the talking.
7. Eliminate evaluations, opinions, judgments, and analysis.

Let's look at an example of the praise/criticism dilemma. A teacher/ student example is used here, but a similar incident could happen in a business or a hospital or a family.

Before the start of a class, a student says to the teacher, "Can I skip the film today and study? I have to finish my book report by the end of the day. My teacher just gave me the assignment two days ago and I haven't had enough time to get it finished." The teacher says, "I doubt if any teacher would give you that much to do in such a short time. Doesn't sound like you planned too well. I can't allow you to miss the film." Of course, many of the rules are broken in the teacher's response, and we have already learned about the tension created when we don't relate well to another individual's feelings. Remember, we are concerned here with the praise/criticism dilemma. When the teacher said "Doesn't sound like you planned too well," he was, in fact, criticizing. He was on his way to "getting out of touch." When he said "I doubt," he was beginning to add fuel to the fire; he was in the initial stage of the *generation gap*. The tension in the student was increased first by the teacher failing to pick up the all important feeling (anxious, swamped, overwhelmed, rushed, pressed) and second by criticizing. The rules broken are: Rule 1, the teacher responded to an event, not feeling; Rule 2, no feeling word was used; Rule 4, the teacher used logic and made an assumption; and Rule 7, gave an opinion and judgment. The possibility of conflict is drawing ever closer!

Let's look at another example. Suppose a mother had been waiting a long time for her son to be seen at an out-patient clinic. She was weary and upset when the doctor did appear. The destructive behavior which might have resulted from her tired, angry feelings could have come out in many destructive patterns such as short, curt answers to the physician's questions. But the physician said to her, "You look tired, you must have been waiting an awfully long time." By saying this to the mother, the physician showed that he was trying to understand how the mother felt and the mother had less of a need to communicate her feelings in ways that might be destructive. The teacher in the example could have applied the same form of communication and eliminated a possible disagreement (Anthony and Carkhuff, 1976, p. 43).

The teacher, in an attempt to avoid conflict could have said something like "It does sound as though you are anxious about your book report. Although you do seem swamped it is very important for us to see the film this period." This approach has a much better chance of preventing conflict. The student's ego is not bruised, his self-esteem is not attacked, he is not doubted, and as Jess Lair so aptly described it, the student was not "given a wall to bounce his ball off of" (Lair, 1969). He was "given a wall to bounce his ball off of" when his feelings were minimized, when he was criticized, evaluated, judged, and responded to in a discouraging manner.

Dr. Lair also pointed out that "acceptance does not mean approval" (Lair, 1969, p. 164). The student's request was not a reasonable one, but even though the teacher might not approve, he could have accepted the feeling. Accepting takes quick evaluation of our own feelings, and by not allowing them to take over we can begin to "get ourselves out of the way."

Blamers and Criticizers

A nonblaming, more encouraging attitude can be developed by most of us in our communication if we take time to observe that a blaming approach rarely works to keep a relationship going (Losoncy, 1977). The teacher became a "blamer" when he used the word "you." What he was really saying was "You should have known better" (Gordon, 1977). The fact is, we should know better! We should know that no matter how we sweeten up the words, most people don't like to be told their behavior is unacceptable (Gordon, 1977).

As we can surmise, the blamer is rarely effective in preventing problems. Blamers widen the relationship gap. Just as with the categories of questioners, evaluators, judgers, minimizers, and so forth, we can fall into the categories which might be labeled "blamers" or "criticizers." To avoid these two categories we should try to remember that encouragement is the factor that brings change (Losoncy, 1977). Encouragement helps stabilize relationships. For the most part positions containing any criticism are ineffective in maintaining tranquility. They are positions that always bring about "discouraging words." They are attempts to dominate and we might consider that domination is force. And when we recall that "we can't make anybody do anything," we see that domination stifles growth (Losoncy, 1977). It stifles communication. It is discouraging!

Hopefully, the material up to now, applied in a conscientious manner, will teach us that empathy and sensitivity are the most important ingredients in the encouragement process (Losoncy, 1977). Most likely they are the most important in the "relationship process." Losoncy offered us some evidence when he suggested that we ask kindergarten children how they like school and then ask senior high school students the same question. He asked, "What happens along the way to people to make them lose the naturalness, enthusiasm, and desire for growth so commonly associated with youth?" He then suggested that people develop this more calcified trend partially as a result of *insensitive social relationships* (Losoncy, 1977, p. 50). I would like to submit that these insensitive social relationships are a result of our LLPs which include the praise/criticism dilemma. The young people being discussed here have had their *future energy* and *enthusiasm* thwarted.

It is easily seen that criticism, breaking our rules, and generally making discouraging remarks (LLPs) can dampen spirits and cause relationships to suffer. But what about praise? What part does praise play in this praise/criticism dilemma?

We must understand first and foremost that praise is important. Total lack of it is devastating to growth and promotion of relationships. However, we have already pointed out that there are times when we praise and we could be picking up feeling as well. This concept is important for us to remember because it helps release us from the praise/criticism dilemma. We can overpraise! Too much praise may cause feelings to be repressed and, as we well know, repressed feelings can cause all kinds of physical and psychological problems. Repression of feelings, good or bad, can cause discouragement. If someone is proud, elated, excited, pleased, contented, delighted, gratified, inspired, jovial, satisfied, thrilled, or whatever, and we seldom plug ourselves in to these feelings, it can be very discouraging for the person expressing these feelings. The same goes for unpleasant feelings. Therein lies the creation and hence the danger of the praise/criticism dilemma. If we praise we may miss the feeling being sent to us; if we criticize we are sure to miss it. Our society has understood that praise is important, as in school, the business world, and parenting methods, but we are just now discovering how we overuse praise and run into difficulty in our attempts to provide growth and development and maintain or establish relationships.

So we must give consideration to the idea that praise and criticism are, at times, ineffective. They are LLPs used *to fill the gap* and often start the resentment cycle. Like pinball machines, praise and criticism are delicate instruments and can be tilted so severely that the sign comes on "game over."

An Equation for Human Development

In this modern era where nearly everything seems to be explained by some formula, equation, computer analysis, systematic approach, or what have you, it still seems unlikely that one could explain human development in technical terms. Nonetheless, void of technical know-how and white-coated assistants, an attempt is made here to create such an equation.

$$\left(\frac{\text{Good Communication-Praise}}{\text{feelings}} \; \frac{}{\text{Poor Communication-Criticism}} \right) = \left(\frac{\text{Encouraged-Independent}}{\text{Discouraged-Dependent}} \right)^{\overparen{\text{Constructive criticism}}} = \left(\frac{\text{Good Human Development}}{\text{Poor Human Development}} \right)$$

It is not my intention to turn this explanation into a math problem or deep-thinking session and tax your mind with the usual technical jargon our society has succumbed to, but the equation may assist some readers in understanding what good communication can do in terms of bringing about human development and establishing meaningful relationships. Remember, most of what is being written here is based on research, so an equation doesn't seem inappropriate.

We can look at the equation as sort of a summing up of that which has been learned so far. We learned in the first three chapters which has been learned so far. We learned in the first three chapters that much of our everyday communication, our LLPs, may be ineffective in our attempts "to keep in touch." We learned that understanding feelings and relating to them is important to growth and development. In the last few pages we learned the importance of the role praise and criticism play and how errors in communication cause discouragement. In the overall analysis we could say that our LLPs cause discouragement and poor self-development of those we are trying to help develop, but also we must say that our LLPs cause people to become discouraged with each other even though they are not trying to help develop each other. They may be just trying to "keep in touch" and maintain a relationship.

The equation can be read as: Good communication, involving picking up feeling and the use of praise with constructive criticism equals an encouraged, independent person which equals good human development (good human relationships). Poor communication, with lack of feeling, improper balance of praise and criticism equals a discouraged-dependent person which equals poor human development (poor human relationships). Notice the little cloud of constructive criticism floating over the top part of the equation. This is included so readers will not get the idea that criticism is taboo.

Earn the Right

Although I think the saying "Quick to criticize, slow to praise," fits our LLPs, we must have criticism of some type. What type? Well, when we criticize we confront, and confrontation and the effects of it are not well understood. The type of criticism or confronting that is most effective is that which takes place in a previously established relationship. It may be beneficial to add to our collection of communication skills the idea that we *must earn the right to confront someone* (Anthony and Carkhuff, 1976). It is my opinion that even after the relationship is well established "confronting abuse" can move the relationship back to the stage where it must be re-established. Far too many relationships, such as a marriage or employer and employee, become strained because after a period of years one side takes for granted that their confrontations will "wear off" or "not have much ill effect" on the person being confronted. There is a point of no return where confrontations, just as overuse of questions, are for our benefit and not the benefit of the person we are confronting.

Socrates said an unexamined life isn't worth living (Lair, 1969, p. 231). Confrontations and criticism certainly lend themselves to this philosophy. If confrontations are not applied with some skill, there is danger that the person being confronted or criticized will dwell on why the person is criticizing rather than actually looking at the behavior that is being criticized. Timing, probably meaning a few times few and far between, is essential when applying criticism. The criticism has more of a chance to be meaningful, to be constructive to growth if discouraging words are not used. Let's look at an example.

Suppose a "boss" says to an employee, "You are going to have to start getting your reports in on time. You are holding things up! I am going to have to do something drastic to help you remember how important this is." This is a confrontation. Many bosses are only concerned about getting results and this communication approach will often get the results wanted now, but creates more problems in the future. A better approach might be, "I've noticed some of your reports have been late recently. Is there something we can do to help?" This approach carries with it a less threatening, a more encouraging message and increases the chances of solving the original problem. It is important for the attitude of the employee in future interactions with the boss. It is also important for the attitude of the employee as he goes about his work. He will not be as enthusiastic working for an employer who uses the discouraging approach as one who forgets his LLPs and seems "to care." Actually most of us do care but our LLPs give off the message that we don't; and then we don't understand why things go awry. So praise, criticism, and "discouraging words" must now be considered potentially dangerous LLPs since used with discretion, they're not automatically evil.

Power in Communication

There is another element in these last examples that must be discussed. We can see the discouraging, blaming, critical approach in them, but a hidden, more subtle error in communication is the use of power.

Dr. Thomas Gordon, author of *Parent Effectiveness Training* and *Leadership Effectiveness Training,* said a person has power when he or she possesses the means to deprive others of something they need (Gordon, 1977, p. 156). He goes on to say:

> The actual exercise of power involves some action that causes others to behave in a certain way despite their oppositions to it—it makes them do something they otherwise would not do. The term psychologists generally use for the "means to deprive others" is "punishment" because to be deprived of something we want very much is felt as punishing. "If you don't do what I want, then I will deprive you of something you need." The use of this source of power is *coercive,* for the recipient feels coerced into compliance with the leader's solution (Gordon, 1977 p. 156).

Much of our communication, unbeknownst to us, contains "power messages." These messages are originated from our LLPs and are discouraging in content. "I'll have to dock your pay," or "We will transfer you to another department," or "If you mess up the drill one more time, you will run fifty laps." It is better for the coach to say, "I know we can do the drill correctly and together, keep trying." This method of teaching is not so critical, it is more encouraging and doesn't embarrass anyone. Also the power factor is removed. Forced compliance is a communication technique that is used daily in our attempts to communicate, but it causes more problems than it solves. If we don't treat others equally, we merely forestall conflicts until a future time.

Most LLPs contain some element of power and are used daily in schools, families, and in the business world. These power LLPs are ineffective! Just as do other type LLPs, they get solutions *now* and create problems *later.* The "power differential," as Gordon so expertly labeled it, is decreasing steadily in most organizations (Gordon, 1977, p. 157). Another way of explaining this is, of course, that power LLPs, the usual form of communication, cause friction and people in the organization or family do what they can to equalize the devastating power LLPs. Leaders, including teachers and parents, would do well to consider the idea that "to influence people without using power is the key to leader effectiveness" (Gordon 1977, p. 8). My belief is that our seven rules will also help eliminate power LLPs or the "power attitude" many leaders still cling to. The days where decisions are made solely by leaders, mandated by power LLPs, and begrudgingly implemented by "subordinates" are numbered. Effective leaders of the future will understand they can lead without the followers knowing they are being led. After all, we only lead by the consent and cooperation of the masses. Our rules and understanding of the total concept of communication described in these pages can assist leaders in developing this attitude of influence, not coercion.

Power then is generated by improper communication techniques. We might apply here the old saying, "If we don't have time to do it right, when will we have the time to do it over?" Every power LLP we use in our attempt to help a child develop, motivate an employee, maintain a friendship, or even sell a used car or keep a marriage together may cause us to have to use time to go back and re-establish our privilege, not a right, to confront or criticize someone. Here again, the use of power in a well established relationship may occur, but we must become able to recognize when our power LLPs are having an undesirable effect . . . before it is too late!

If leaders do not recognize these signs as to their ineffectiveness in the communication process, alienation occurs, relationships deteriorate, and as Dr. Gordon explained, this is why so many leaders "feel alone at the top" (Gordon, 1977, p. 167). Some refer to this unwanted phenomenon as "the loneliness of command." At any rate, the leader's power has been diminished and "those in charge" have few people with whom to really relate except those people who have not been victims of their power LLPs.

One of the real problems with current communication techniques is how our LLPs take us away from the chance of relaying good, positive information we have about someone. The use of power creates messages negative in tone as does misuse of praise and criticism. If we can learn to relay feelings and positive information, we won't need to use power in communication to accomplish tasks. We can create congenial, healthy, psychologically sound environments in schools, families, and businesses. Losoncy vividly pointed out, "Positive information you have about a person is meaningless unless it is communicated to that person" (Losoncy, 1977, p. 52). Positive information cannot be relayed by indulging in all of the improper communication techniques discussed so far. It must be relayed to a person "so they know that you know."

A perfect example of positive information not being sent back to someone is where a youngster brings home a report card with three As, a B, and a C, and the youngster's parents *first* notice the C. Yes, we too often get it backwards, and somehow we must learn to reverse this trend. Is it the negativism of the human species brought about by our LLPs that causes this trend? I think so. We have *learned* to use the negative approach to motivate. We try to provide growth and get things done by the use of power communication. It simply doesn't work!

The use of power in communication is so prevalent that it must be included in our equation, for minus factors are as important as plus factors in equations. So adding power as a minus factor in our equation for good communication and human development, the equation should now look something like this:

$$\left(\frac{\text{Good Communication-Praise}}{\text{Poor Communication-Criticism}} \text{-feelings-} \right) \begin{array}{l} \text{minus} \\ \text{power} \end{array} = \left(\frac{\text{Encouraged-Independent}}{\text{Discouraged-Dependent}} \right) = \left(\frac{\text{Good Human Development}}{\text{Poor Human Development}} \right)$$

Constructive criticism

So we can see the elimination of power messages and negative words can be accomplished by dwelling on the positive things different people present to us. Failing to accomplish this, we cause those around us to lose confidence. As Losoncy explained, "Once people lose confidence, their whole approach to life changes. Their facial expression, their walk, and even their goals in life come to show their negative self-image" (Losoncy, 1977, p. 25). We seldom look at communication as the real culprit that brings about this state in an individual. I have been intrigued about this phenomenon for nearly twenty years in working with people. Finally, the common denominator, the communication process, made itself clear to me. It became clear because power, criticism, coercion, discouraging words, blame, minimized feelings, and all the other errors in communication so often became the prime force, the major ingredient in the lives of people who had continued problems.

Losoncy noted that "Lack of confidence is brought about by

Ridicule and failure pushed boy to kill himself

by Al Rossiter Jr.

WASHINGTON (UPI) — Danny was an 18-year-old who had suffered epileptic seizures several times a month for 10 years.

His intelligence was considered "borderline," and the best grades he could get were C's and D's. He dropped out of school after the 11th grade and eventually was encouraged to enroll in a different school to qualify for a vocational rehabilitation program.

The young man found it hard to adjust to the new school. His aggressive personality offended classmates and teachers, and he had no real friends. Since he was mentally slow, physically uncoordinated and prone to seizures during school, he was an outcast.

His teachers did not know him well, and his school counselor ignored him.

Danny did not find much support at home. His father, a truck driver, ridiculed him, accusing Danny of violent and anti-social behavior. His older sister fought with him and provoked more seizures.

DANNY FINALLY moved in with an older brother in a different town. That added to his isolation.

He was frustrated by school failure and was unable to see any hope for the future. Shortly before Christmas, Danny hung himself.

"Danny's suicide was a result of many factors," said Dr. David L. Coulter of the University of Michigan Medical Center at Ann Arbor, "but his handicaps were the primary factors that determined his life.

> Danny's environment had programmed him for failure. It gave him few chances to succeed in building self-esteem — instead, it promoted frustration and feelings of worthlessness.

"No matter how hard he tried, he could never succeed in school, and other children ridiculed his failure. There was no arena of personal accomplishment, such as athletics, that could have provided him with a sense of worth.

"His intellectual limitation also restricted his ability to see beyond the concrete reality of his difficult life and obtain insight into his feelings of despair. He was ridiculed in school for having seizures, and his family regarded his epilepsy as a sign that he was worthless."

Coulter related this account in the Sept. 12 issue of the Journal of the American Medical Assn. He said many adolescents face similar situations.

Coulter said Danny's environment had programmed him to failure. It gave him few chances to succeed in building self-esteem, promoting instead frustration and feelings of worthlessness.

"SOME CHILDREN are so overwhelmed by this sense of worthlessness that they give up and stop competing in a world where they cannot succeed," Coulter said. "Failure then becomes a self-fulfilling prophecy."

He said children with handicaps that prevent success need help from health professionals and educators to change their environment and help them learn how to cope.

"These children derive what strength they can from family and friends," he said, "but live in stages of despair.

"If we are to help them, we must begin to recognize the unfairness of their lives and try to help them find successful strategies to cope with a difficult and demanding world."

Reprinted by permission of United Press International.

74

the feelings of inferiority, not inferiority itself" (Losoncy, 1977, p. 28). We all know people who seem to be unaware of a weakness they may have, even though everyone else notices it, but the weakness doesn't adversely affect the behavior of the individual. One of the real problems we face in our society is the one of communicating in such a way that we make people aware of weaknesses. We make people aware of what *we* think is a weakness, but it only becomes a weakness to the individual when he becomes aware that many around him now regard an aspect of his being as a weakness. It wasn't a weakness until our LLPs made it one! We keep applying our LLPs until the weakness begins to affect the individual. We may feel stronger, more powerful, because we make others feel weaker. We could use this energy to build up others and, hence, ourselves. Of course this is not to say that there aren't weaknesses that must be corrected, but there are some that would be better off left alone.

The newspaper article shown on page 74 seems to give some support to the idea that our LLPs can have an adverse effect on people. Danny was a victim of LLPs. His aggressive personality was formed to fight back against LLPs. Danny could find few people who weren't submerged in LLPs rather strongly. Power, discouraging words, the praise/criticism dilemma, and other negative messages all flourished in Danny's short life, and he finally ended it. He escaped from the powerful LLP syndrome. LLPs do often overlook such things as feelings of pride in personal accomplishments that give human beings the sense of self-worth. Danny needed that type input from those around him; he just didn't get it.

Feelings of despair, such as Danny obviously had, should not be *originated* by another person or a group of persons. Despair is brought on often enough by events that occur in our environment. Why do we need to add to it with our LLPs? Everywhere Danny went people were depriving him of an opportunity "to build self-esteem." Can't we relate to the Dannys of the world in a more positive, humane way and help them develop the best they can?

It might be helpful to us here in the discussion of Danny to recall part of the definition of power. It is "The action that causes others to behave in a certain way despite their opposition to it" (Gordon, 1977, p. 156). In the case of Danny, possibly we could say that power LLPs are killers, and it seems safe to say they are very crippling to many who engage in the communication process.

We listed several obstacles in the last three chapters that get in the way of good communication. These obstacles, when not overcome, cause devastating problems in relationships. We have encountered still more obstacles in this chapter and, hopefully, we have become better informed as to the *effects* of our LLPs. It would follow then that we may have come across some more categories that we should try to prevent ourselves from being in when we attempt to communicate. Don't you agree that we often place ourselves in a category we might label as "discouragers?" And what about "praisers/ criticizers?" And would you accept "blamers?" And didn't Danny have "ridiculers" in his short life?

List of Categories

Our list of categories has become awesome! It may be that as we read about them we tell ourselves, "OK, I do that once in a while, but I'm not so bad." The "awesomeness" may be minimized by the scattered explanations. So, since the purpose of this chapter is, in part, designed to help us understand the overall effects of our LLPs, it seems it might be effective to list, all in one tight, concise package, the communication categories we find ourselves in most everyday. The list reveals those things we do that promote deterioration of human relationships.

LIST OF CATEGORIES

Blamers	Discouragers	Praisers/Criticizers
Ridiculers	Advicers	Deprivers
Solutioners	Suggestioners	Judgers
Analyzers	Evaluators	Concluders
Minimizers	Persuaders	Moralizers
Questioners	Probers	Investigators
Anticipators	Assumptionists	Interveners

Body Language

I can think of only one other factor that can affect relationships or human development and that factor is body language. There are several good books on the market about body language or "attending behavior." Those wishing to add even more to their ability to "keep in touch" could benefit by reading a few of them.

It is not quite enough to master the skills and techniques in this book. We must understand that our bodies give off LLP messages. We are taught these LLPs, or rather they are ingrained in us just as our verbal LLPs are ingrained within us. Facial expressions, movements that are designed to ignore someone, eye contact or lack of it, and other body LLPs are learned. We often deliver a message more with our bodies than with our mouths. It's possible to scream out with our mouths closed and still deliver our LLPs. A shrug or a smirk used at the wrong time can be considered an LLP. Our body LLPs may be even more devastating and have more effect than our verbal LLPs. Body LLPs and verbal LLPs probably helped Danny to decide to kill himself. We need to bring both type LLPs to a more conscious level in upgrading human relations. Lest we forget "the gap," the relationship gap can be started by body LLPs.

It is almost an overwhelming task to view the awesome list of categories on the last page and think, "We need to eliminate a lot of those in our communication systems, and now we are reminded that our bodies deliver LLPs also." It would seem we need to improve because as we discover in the next chapter, our LLPs have a great effect on the three segments of our society that include the vast majority of people . . . families, education, and business.

References

ANTHONY, WILLIAM and CARKHUFF, ROBERT R. *The Art of Health Care.* Amherst, Mass.: Human Resource Developmental Press, Inc., 1976.

GORDON, THOMAS. *L.E.T. Leader Effectiveness Training.* Reprinted with permission of Wyden Books from *L.E.T. Leader Effectiveness Training* by Dr. Thomas Gordon. Copyright (c) 1977 by Dr. Thomas Gordon.

LAIR, JESS. *"I Ain't Much Baby—But I'm All I've Got.* New York: Fawcett Publications, Inc. 1969, 1972. (Doubleday and Company).

LOSONCY, LEWIS. *Turning People On: How to Be an Encouraging Person.* (c) 1977. Reprinted by permission of Prentice-Hall, Inc., Englewood Cliffs, New Jersey.

five

Communication Skills in Education, Parenting, and Business

In the past few years I have heard and read a great deal about humanizing education. Addressing itself to the problem, the Office of Health, Education, and Welfare reported that research indicated that more than half of the students interviewed said their teachers were not very interested in them. Others studies have shown that teachers interaction with students lacked a positive tone. I'm sure nearly every teacher would deny the charge of unconcern, but when two sides disagree there is usually some fault on both sides. Although most teachers are concerned about the well-being of their students, their concern apparently is not being conveyed to them.

The Gallup polls have long revealed that discipline is the number one problem in the nation's schools. (See the chart on page 80.) A recent Gallup poll also defined "better teachers" as those who try to understand each student's problems. The ideas presented in the first four chapters of this book reveal a look behind the scenes at what really causes "poor discipline and poor teaching" in our schools. Rest assured improper listening and responding is a major, if not the number one, factor. Despite a large amount of evidence that suggests that the communication problem is at the root of school problems, not much is being done about it. Institutions incorporating

WHAT'S WRONG WITH THE SCHOOLS?

Lack of discipline is viewed as the biggest problem facing the public schools today, according to a recent Gallup opinion poll. Twenty-five percent of Americans cited lack of discipline in the schools as a major problem with which communities must deal. The use of drugs, lack of financial support for the schools, integration and busing, and poor curriculum and poor standards were among the top ten ranked problems.

When asked what, if anything, could be done to improve education, those interviewed suggested stricter discipline, better teachers, more emphasis on the "basics," more parental involvement, and higher scholastic standards.

Better teachers were defined as those teachers who take a personal interest in each student and who try to understand each student's problems. Good teachers, according to the survey, were those who encourage students to achieve good grades and who inspire students to set high goals for themselves.

The results of the entire poll, which included questions across a broad range of educational issues, are printed in *Phi Delta Kappan* magazine (September 1978). Reprints are available (minimum order twenty-five copies for $5.50) from: Phi Delta Kappa, Inc., Box 789, Bloomington, IN 47401.

Americans listed the following problems in response to the question, "What do you think are the biggest problems with which the public schools in this community must deal?"

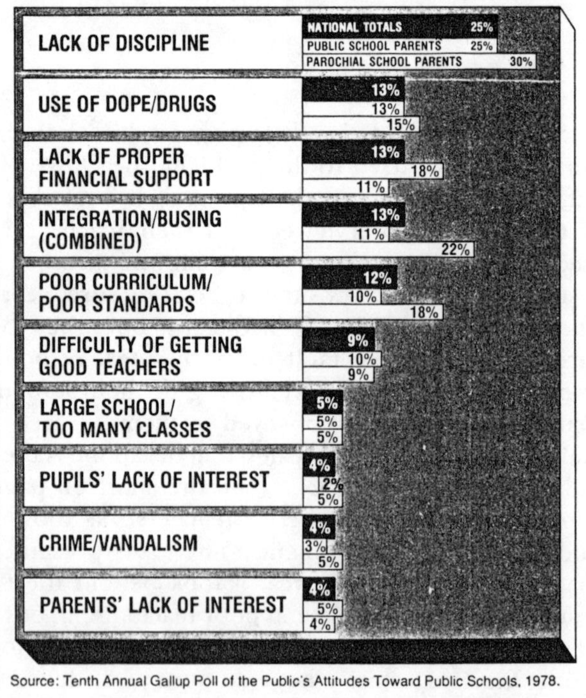

Source: Tenth Annual Gallup Poll of the Public's Attitudes Toward Public Schools, 1978.

Reprinted with permission from the American Educator, Winter, 1978, p. 5.

these skills could soon enjoy improved cooperation between students and teachers because we know that we can teach people to become more empathetic. We should emphasize instruction in communication skills in our schools. This instruction has been shown to be important to human development and we now have the tools to begin this educational process.

Humanizing Education

Of course, just the idea that much has been written about humanizing education suggests that it *is not* very humanistic. To my way of thinking the desirable transformation to a more person-oriented system has little to do with architecture, automation, curriculum, more money, teachers and administrators taking advanced courses, or even high-powered PTA meetings or teachers' meetings. These factors are not as important as educators identifying and then doing something about the devastatingly harmful communication process which causes the dehumanization in the nation's schools. The common communication obstacles and categories identified in the last chapter are the real ingredients that people are writing about when they write about the "dehumanization process in American schools." The three Rs, reading, 'riting, and 'rithmetic are well known. We should add the fourth R . . . relating!

Humanistic education cannot be approached, though, until our society does three things: (1) Train *all* professional educators and others who work in schools in interpersonal communications skills, (2) Train *all* parents in these skills so their children will not take out their frustrations (of not being heard) at school, (3) Train students in the early years as to how to communicate properly. Of course, a complete change is impossible, but we can do much, much more than we are doing at the present time.

For example, at present when a teacher comes out of college it seems we give him or her a gradebook, chalk, some textbooks, and thirty-five students in a class or 150 students a day and hope for the best results. Some teachers are empathetic: most are "ordinary men" (Egan, 1975) as far as interpersonal communication skills are concerned. Colleges and universities could, and should, include a required course in interpersonal communication for all teachers. Actually, such a course requirement for all graduates would be better. Won't most of these graduates become parents, teachers, and businesspeople?

On the other hand, I don't believe we can place all of the blame on the universities at this point. The fact is we are just now learning what should and should not be said to young people in terms of development. Research of the type mentioned at the start of this book will, I believe, someday become conclusive enough to convince leaders in education, and those in psychology who determine the direction of our schools, that humanizing can only be accomplished by humans relating better to one another. Is that so difficult to figure out? I see little evidence to make the future look brighter when I hear of schools wanting to upgrade their communications, and the educators talk about PA announcements, written communications, organizing brochures, and so forth. These are necessary items, but interpersonal communications are the source of attitude problems with teachers, students, and parents. Relationship problems can seldom be solved by streamlining the PA system or curriculum brochures.

Educators can be taught these skills, but education probably changes more slowly than any other organization or business in our country. This inability to change is not very encouraging when we think of the immediate need to humanize schools and upgrade education.

The generation gap alluded to earlier and depersonalized schools have a great deal in common. Students want teachers who are sensitive to their feelings. They want teachers who are good listeners. Often times we have young people in our classrooms who don't care how much we know; they simply want to know how much we care. These youngsters *begin* their communication processes with feelings, not with words. The feelings come first; the words are sporadic attempts to get their feelings out. The caring is more important to them than knowledge because they are verbally and possibly physically abused children. When this empathy and interest (not curiosity) is apparent, the student learns in a good psychological atmosphere. Aren't educators supposed to address themselves to the emotional needs of their students as well as the educational needs?

It seems that educators are at least somewhat responsible for helping young adults make an effective entrance into the adult world.

They can accomplish this more readily by looking at how some teachers make people feel understood, capable, useful, encouraged, worthwhile, and happy rather than uncomfortable, discouraged, nervous, bored, or incapable. Intimidation in terms of fear, coercion, sarcasm, criticism, humiliation, and discouraging remarks is often applied in the classrooms, labs, and athletic fields, but it is seldom an effective motivator. Somehow we must encourage those teachers, coaches, administrators, counselors, secretaries, and others who continue to use their LLPs, to look for more effective methods that convey confidence and respect. Rather than coercing students to go along with the "establishment" we can earn their support and gain their respect and cooperation and be happy while teaching and learning go on. Why can't we use the "ear" in *learning*, listen to the students, and then respond more effectively?

Far too often teachers solve problems, but the communication method used causes the relationship to suffer. It solves the problem for the teacher and administration, but not for the student. Solutions of this type are not worth demolishing a relationship between a teacher and a student (Lillibridge, 1977).

As we can see in our misuse of logic, current methods used to correct misbehavior are the real reasons why the student's behavior stays the same or even worsens. We can begin to ferret out these common, accepted, but ineffective methods and substitute a better form of communication. "We are too mistake-oriented," is a comment often heard in education. However, it doesn't seem that educators really know how mistakes in attempting to change behavior are really made. The solution to humanizing the schools can be seen a little more clearly if we would only set up a system to help people recognize poor communication habits (LLPs) and then help them refine their listening and responding skills. People must experience better methods and see the results before they will consider changing.

It is well known that education employs a large number of people in our society. These people help develop personalities which, in turn, eventually influence thousands of other personalities. This makes it clear that educators touch many, many lives in our country. We can see that the inability to respond to feeling by a teacher, may hinder intellectual, as well as emotional, growth. We have known for some time that empathy, positive regard, and genuineness are related to intellectual achievement as well as emotional and psycholog-ical development.[1] If the student seems to be worse off in adjusting to life, school, and society in general, part of the trouble may be traced to the front of the classroom, to the teacher, rather than to the student.

Over the years I have sought meaningful definitions in education. In regard to humanizing the schools through more effective communi-cations I would submit the following: First, I believe good teaching is the ability to inspire learning. We can only inspire people by the example we set and by the way we respond to them . . . much of the inspiration needed today is undermined by the way we say things to students. We transmit our expectations, opinions, criticism, values, advice, ideas, and solutions, unknowingly, too often, and at the wrong time. This serves only to discourage young people, especially when we attack their self-esteem. It is particularly disturbing to discover that these attacks on self-esteem occur because it is well documented that satisfaction with self is an important item in the development of good mental health. Development of this self-satisfaction helps to motivate a student to utilize his academic potential.

Second, I believe education should be development of people along with academic achievement. Are we, in the way we respond, developing students in such a way that they can make a respectable transference to adulthood and the world of work? Are we developing young people so they will think independently?

The outstanding teachers inspire learning *and* develop people because they have above average interpersonal communication skills, good knowledge of subject matter, desire to teach, and a sense of fairness. The poor teachers have an overwhelming need to "heap their stuff" on their students. By improper responding, teachers often convey a superior attitude and make students feel inferior. The stu-dents will have some information punched into them by these teachers, but my view is that the information will not be very well retained because the classroom atmosphere was not all that pleasant to be in. The student's attitude is "Let's just get it over with." Poor re-sponses cause disruptive classrooms that certainly develop noisy, de-

[1] From *Beyond Counseling and Therapy* by Robert R. Carkhuff and Bernard G. Beren-son. Copyright © 1967 by Holt, Rinehart and Winston, Inc. Reprinted by permission of Holt, Rinehart and Winston.

structive, abusive children. Where morale is high, learning can take place.

Recognizing individual differences, being understanding, caring, and tolerant, as well as possessing compassion and enthusiasm, are all characteristics that good teachers can develop through learning better communication skills.

From my perspective, a teacher should possess skills that encourage students to do their best, to try. The acquisition of interpersonal communication skills is unlimited in its possibilities to motivate students, to inspire them to do their best. Also, I think acquisition of these skills increases the possibility for longer, more enjoyable teaching careers because many student problems can be handled more effectively once the skills are mastered. It seems certain many problems can be prevented because so many are actually caused by a poor response.

It is clear that many in education simply deny the past. They fail to see that their past responses have been ineffective or harmful, not knowing there is a more acceptable way to communicate. As with many people experiencing problems, they are comfortable with their unawareness. It takes work to improve!

A suggestion I would like to make to all those in education is that some depth be added to what they are doing. Ask, "How long has it been since I really examined any teaching habits and especially my verbal responses?" The things that have been accomplished up to now need not be the standards for tomorrow. Do, however, try to view the learning of these skills as a new opportunity in all of your relationships rather than solely as an obligation in the classroom or office.

Ask also, "How often am I approached by students asking for help?" This may be a clue (not always) as to how much improvement is needed in the relating skills. I have heard many in the field say that a "teacher's moment" comes when the teacher really knows he or she has related well and taught a student something meaningful. The teacher and the student thus experience each other and are communicating. We can create more of these moments by humanizing the schools with better communication skills.

As educators, do we work as well under supervisors, administrators, department heads, and directors if we feel threatened, discouraged, insecure, disillusioned, intimidated, doubtful, and apprehensive? Why then do we expect students to do so? Before talking to your next student, consider how you felt when you were tested, scored, ranked, rated, observed, intimidated, advised, and criticized! (Banville, 1978).

Another way of humanizing the schools through better communications is to ask if we *really* identify the most important elements of the teaching process? Are we trying to encourage or persuade students? Do we respond properly when a student becomes upset, seems unhappy, or acts out to gain attention? Do we try to influence or coerce? Do we cling to our LLPs? It seems that somehow we get the idea that our typical responses are not harmful because the kids are used to them. We get away with poor responses for two reasons: (1) Few people recognize a poor response, and (2) The response has to be nearly an act of negligence before anyone complains.

How often do we examine our responses to one student in a class, then observe what effect the remark had on the entire class? If we break some of our seven rules in front of the class, we must remember the other students are listening and beginning to put us in some of the categories mentioned in the last chapter. How many of these harmful categories can we afford to be in? Can't these ineffective communication patterns affect the *future energy* and *enthusiasm* of students?

Through the use of communication skills teachers can cease to be a part of the problem in schools and become an integral part of the solution. The benefits of these skills certainly exceed any liabilities they might carry. We must, as educators, realize that our words and actions are powerful forces.

It seems imperative that educators incorporate into the schools recent research regarding communication skills. We can rid ourselves of verbal "muggings" and steadfastly strive to provide a climate which will encourage individuals to become more self-directing. We can cease to malign self-esteem and inadequacies in students, stop interjecting inferiority in them, and become more effective in helping them to become happy, effective citizens.

Summing up my thoughts on humanizing education by using better communication skills, I include a quote by Albert Einstein. "It is in fact nothing short of a miracle that modern methods of instruction have not yet entirely strangled the holy curiosity of inquiry. . . . It is a very grave mistake to think that enjoyment of seeing and searching can be promoted by means of coercion and a sense of duty" (Driekurs and Cassel, 1972, p. 51).

Parents and Communication

Although it is easy to find articles, TV programs, and books on the subject of humanizing the schools, it appears that more active work is actually being done on humanizing families. Classes for parents have been organized all over the country. Parent Effectiveness Training, S.T.E.P. (Systematic Training for Effective Parenting), and other organizations offer parents skills in building relationships. These classes seem to be more available than teachers' classes offering similar content.

To be certain, I believe learning good discipline procedures, holding family meetings, and understanding child behavior are important in the parenting process, but chances of these things being effective can be enhanced with the addition of good interpersonal skills. To me, excluding them is like trying to start your car without the key. If family members learn not to break the rules offered earlier in this book, they can have constructive family meetings and negotiations.

Obviously, we still have a long way to go to humanize homes, but an effort seems to have started. Perhaps we have recognized the fact that parents are often blamed for their children's behavior and have finally begun to offer training in proper methods of parenting (Gordon, 1970). Many classes are offered now for expectant couples, but the day must come when we realize that most parents need help with discipline and communication techniques that reach well beyond the infant years. There is more to parenting than keeping diapers clean!

Our society demands credentials for educators, but few (other than a blood test) for parents. As parents, we seldom look at our own dehumanizing behavior; rather, it seems easier to criticize our children's behavior or believe, as some do, that science is dehumanizing us. *We* are dehumanizing ourselves! We don't often search for evidence that might suggest we are not doing well. The three headings (shown below) appeared in the *Chicago Tribune the same day!* Possible evidence!

Somehow we must create an attitude, as the P.E.T. and the S.T.E.P. classes attempt to do, that children and adults are equal in human worth and dignity (Dinkmeyer and McKay, 1976). Life-long patterns (LLPs) are the real cause of child abuse, and we must consider the fact that while physical abuse is the only abuse given much publicity, it is not the only abuse. It is easier to see a bruised body than a bruised mind. The verbal abuse, as we have noted in earlier chapters, is even worse. As Dr. Clark Moustakas beautifully stated, "Nothing is more devastating than the continual experience of not being listened to, not being recognized or understood" (Moustakas, 1975, p. 1).

Often these tragic lives are the results of poor family backgrounds. Not always, but more often than not, these lives are symptomatic of poor communication within a family for personality development is enhanced by good interpersonal communication in the child's environment. Usually no one recognizes what is actually happening to the family and its members until it is too late. These unhappy lives are led by discouraged people, and I believe the inability

Child-abuse murders increasing; legislator calls for state probe

Man charged in the beating death of boy on West Side

18   Section 1   Chicago Tribune. Sunday. April 23. 1978

Wife's nightmare: He beat, then killed 3 children in fire

to give them "human nourishment"[2] in the way of listening and responding by someone prominent in their lives is a major cause of discouragement and disillusionment. And are we going to see more newspaper articles such as the one below?

Man, 25, sues mom, dad for parenting malpractice

BOULDER, Colo. (UPI) — Tom Hansen doesn't think his prents raised him properly. He feels so strongly about it he's suing them for $350,000 in damages.

Hansen, 25, filed suit in district court Wednesday against his father, Richard Hansen of Kilo, Hawaii, and mother, Shirley Hansen of Boulder.

The suit said Hansen will require psychiatric care the rest of his life because of the manner in which he was raised.

HANSEN'S LAWYER, John Taussig Jr., said the suit alleges the parents were guilty of willful and wanton neglect.

"Basically, what we are doing is bringing a suit for malpractice of parenting," Taussig said.

The suit said Hansen's parents neglected his needs for food, clothing, shelter and psychological support at crucial periods of his life. It said he was forced at the age of 14 to "work long hours at menial labor on little food."

When he was 14, Hansen said he was suspended from school while the family was living in Kamuela, Hawaii, where his father worked as a scientist.

HIS FATHER treated him as a "social outcast, subjecting him to humiliation and ridicule and physically attacking him," the suit said.

Taussig said he believes parents should be held responsible for damage to the physical and mental health of their children.

The suit seeks $250,000 in medical expenses and $100,000 in punitive damages.

Reprinted by permission of United Press International.

Abuse promotes abuse! Violence promotes violence! Children learn from abuse to abuse themselves by becoming dropouts, delinquents, prostitutes, drug addicts, thieves, alcoholics, and suicide victims. Such life styles mentioned above are attempts by abused people to belong, to affiliate with someone or something worthwhile to them, for they have been left out all their lives by having their feelings rejected by the people closest to them.

We *all* have a basic need to belong. So often we, as adults,

[2] From *Beyond Counseling and Therapy* by Robert R. Carkhuff and Bernard G. Berenson. Copyright © 1967 by Holt, Rinehart and Winston, Inc. Reprinted by permission of Holt, Rinehart and Winston.

tell kids they don't belong by the way we respond to them. We often make kids feel inferior, insecure, or inadequate, when we compare them to each other or miss hearing their feelings.

Recently, I have become convinced that our young people become vulnerable because of our inability to communicate at a feeling level. The discouragement and disillusionment instilled by LLPs runs deeper than we realize. Evidence is all around us, but we cover it up. Please allow me to explain my use of the term vulnerability.

A mother called me and related that her daughter had been "captured" by the "Moonie cult" in California. Although the girl was now safe, the mother was having some difficulty understanding how her daughter could have been overwhelmed by members of a cult. What happened to her daughter's ability to reason? Why was she so vulnerable? The girl was attractive, an excellent student, active in school, and well-liked. She possessed the All-American characteristics. The mother and I talked about the situation, and she gave me some information about "cults." Interestingly, in one of the articles Rabbi Davis of the Jewish Community Center in White Plains, New York, was discussing how personality-destroying cults can, within a short time, capture a person's mind and all of his or her earthly belongings and money. Rabbi Davis asked, "What's missing? What causes this susceptibility in our nation's young people?" And can this same susceptibility continue into adulthood? Recently there was the shocking holocaust of 900 deaths, many suicides, in Jonestown, Guyana. This cult included many in *older* age groups!

I certainly do not claim to have the single answer as to what causes seemingly good people to become vulnerable and overwhelmed by cults. I do firmly believe, though, that these people become vulnerable because feelings have been overlooked. LLPs were ever present in their background, the "gap" was not filled properly and not filled often enough by significant people in their lives, not just by parents, but by many people. That is what's missing! That is what causes some of the vulnerability. The way we communicate is a partial answer to Rabbi Davis's question. Kids often don't know who they are because parents and others don't have the communication skills to help them discover who they are.

I explained to the confused mother and her daughter my ideas about how our communication skills are an intricate part of the difficulty they experienced in California. Young people, unsure as to who they are or where they are going, are looking for ways to discover answers. As Rabbi Davis suggested, "They hunger for acceptance." If anyone, just anyone hears their feelings, fills the "gap" with a meaningful response, or shows some understanding, they will follow that person.

After the Jonestown debacle I read in the *Chicago Tribune* that a psychiatrist who interviewed the survivors made a discovery that seemed to verify what I am discussing here. The psychiatrist, an expert on cults, stated that many of the people he talked to *were not in touch with their real feelings!* How important feelings are! It isn't difficult to understand that cult leaders and their followers are experts in communicating and picking up feelings. They offer understanding and the chance to be heard. Hitler did it, Jim Jones, Charles Manson, the Reverend Moon, and others were "very understanding" too! Followers "belong" and often need to belong because they didn't "belong" to a few people or at least someone on a deeper feeling level before hand.

Dependency on others, as has been mentioned, is caused by us and unrecognized by us as a problem in our culture. Cults and similar organizations prey on dependent, vulnerable people. Rabbi Davis suggested that we "begin again to listen with our ears and with our hearts." I agree! If we can remove the insulation around our hearts we may be able to relate to feelings a little better. Perhaps then we can begin to understand one another a little better. Perhaps!

Our society, it seems, could do a better job of preparing young people for the "peaks and valleys" of life. Recently I heard someone say, "Why should we lead our kids to believe that someone will always be around to help them arrange their lives?" We simply rescue our young people too much. We take away their attempts at independency, and when *we* think the time is right, we give it back to them and say, "You are independent now." Then we get upset because the kids don't handle their new-found independence too well. We seem to lack the understanding that it is healthy to become independent, as well as the skills to foster independence.

We should teach kids to have a self-identity. We can't lead them all of the time and shouldn't make all of their decisions. When children are led to believe they need a leader all their lives they will probably find one. And, believe me, unscrupulous leaders abound in our society!

Of course, the vulnerability I have been talking about relates to self-esteem, and we promote or prevent development of self-esteem by the verbal patterns we choose to use. Research has shown that girl crimes are related to low self-esteem, and juvenile delinquents are often suffering from poor visions of self-worth. I think we can safely include poor school performance in this category also.

These youngsters are seeking identity and few people are helping them discover it. By practicing the skills of better communication, we may be able to help clarify ambitions, needs, values, feelings, ideas, aspirations, fears, and so on. An important part of any relationship is the meeting of needs. Needs are made evident by expressions of feelings. Needs can't be picked up if feelings are not picked up. Remember, people seldom use the proper feeling word to express their true feeling.

It is difficult for many parents to talk with their children from an internal rather than external frame of reference. "Internal" means real feelings, not secondary; and "external" means what the parents are thinking or how they react to events. "External" viewpoints would correlate with our LLPs. As parents we often respond in a manner that seems to convey the idea we are hoping our youngsters will take on our identity instead of developing their own. Too often the ambitions of our kids reflect our ambitions as parents (Dinkmeyer and McKay, 1976). It bothers me, as a counselor, when I hear a student say, "My mom wants me to__________." Or, "My dad will get mad if I don't go to college at __________." I think much better relationships are going on when I hear, "My folks and I talked it over and I decided to __________."

We spend a great deal of time trying to change other people or persuading people to become like us or someone also equally adept at life. This certainly seems true when we consider that it seems to be a trait in our country that we yell at, push, shake, drag, spank, and shove our kids more than any other country in the world. When parents can't change their kids through these methods, they feel guilty and confused. Uncertainty as to how to handle the situation causes the parents to strike back, usually verbally. There is an attempt, usually a frustrating one, to keep the power in the hands of parents. One of my favorite lines used in teaching parents is "We can't make anyone do anything." Still, we blindly keep using force long after it has proven to be ineffective.

Autocratic or overprotective methods of raising children are the two most common and least effective. Overpermissiveness is as harmful as being too authoritarian. Our LLPs dictate these methods and, to some degree, develop the emotional level in reacting to things the kids say or do. Children who are forced to yield to the power may have adjustment difficulties later in life. Of course, this depends upon how emotionally weak the child becomes. Some telltale signs surfaced during the Second World War when it was concluded by some psychiatrists that the most severely disturbed soldiers were products of over-protective mothers. Adding to this, the song most requested of Bing Crosby when he visited the troops in the South Pacific during World War II was said to be "Brahms Lullaby." (From *Why Am I Afraid to Tell You Who I Am?* by John Powell, S. J. (c) 1969, Argus Communications, Niles, Il. Used with permission.) Let's face it, of all the songs sung by Bing Crosby this was an unusual request and I doubt if we can chalk it up as a coincidence! We must understand that the real world does not cater to such dependency.

"Rather than a parent-molded product, personality now appears to be a nature-given tendency which is revealed as it reacts with environment up until death itself," is an elusive, doubt-casting remark made in the book *The Psychological Society* (Gross, 1978, p. 254). This is leading one to believe "whatever will be, will be." God help us if we ever assume the position that all parenting techniques are good and new techniques cannot help our society develop strong, healthy personalities. It is true parents cannot completely mold a personality, but they can certainly have a great effect on the outcome.

Recently, I viewed a Chicago based TV program entitled *"Project Parenting."* (WBBM-TV Channel 2 Chicago) An ex-gang member was asked what he thought could be done to prevent teenagers from getting on the wrong track in their lives. He said, "Communication, parents communicating better." On the same program a counseling agency worker answered, "Listening, really listening." They know! If personality is nature given, it most certainly can be "parent altered." Good or poor techniques of listening and responding are, in my judgment, more decisive developmental forces regarding the development of children than genetics. Blaming heredity is an easy way out. Are we just to say parents are off the hook? Are we to assume, as the book *The Psychological Society* strongly suggests that "newly developed doubts" (Gross, 1978, p. 248) about the effects of parenting show that heredity will rule no matter what we try to do in helping our kids develop?

These doubts are not new. Why do we deny the evidence around us and cling to the notion that adolescence and teenage tension are genetically mandated and therefore inevitable? I think we can safely say that instead of emotional turbulence that *must* evolve, adolescence tension is a period created by the American social structure (Shertzer and Stone, 1976), . . . and we can do something about it. We can realize, as many psychologists do, that discouragement and poor self-esteem is at the bottom of most misbehavior and rebellion in our adolescence and teens. Our "ingrained special language" (LLPs) is the greatest influence on relationships. If applied correctly, they can provide cohesiveness in relationships.

Dr. Sol Gordon of Syracuse University, who appeared on the *"Project Parenting"* program, encouraged parents to communicate in such a way that they might become "askable" parents. Genetics does not determine whether or not we become "askable." The effects of society, the use of LLPs or lack of them, of those around us help develop "askability." Although predisposed temperament may give a person a "better chance" to communicate well, it can be destroyed by LLPs, particularly when physical and verbal abuse abound.

Another parenting item in the realm of communication, and one I have trouble with, is the idea that we should take out time to spend with our kids. I recently heard a psychologist say that time spent in quantity is not as important as time spent with quality in it. I would like to suggest that quality time is any time good communication is taking place. It is any time we can spend eliminating the generation gap. Keep in mind there is a difference in the giving of time and actually relating. Today, when the economic climate often forces both parents to work, the concept of quality time looms as critical. It seems to me that we simply do not take the feelings of our young people seriously enough. Quality time is the time we should be able to give to our youngsters and let them know, by the way we listen and respond, that we do take their feelings as seriously as our own.

Parents rebuking quality time choose to keep their LLPs and give children the impression that they own them. We can only pay off the mortgage, so to speak, when we *help* them grow rather than *make* them grow.

Being responsible as a parent is decidedly different than taking on parent responsibilities. Parents submit to the pressure of society to *make* their kids behave properly. When they attempt to make them behave without the proper communication skills, the family, and often the community, are faced with unpleasant problems to solve.

It would seem that proper communication techniques are more important in marriages than they used to be. The concept of quality time is important for couples even if they choose not to have children. The married lives of people used to average twenty years; now we often hear of celebrations of fifty years of married life. On the other hand, many people divorce after twenty or thirty years, and some of this has to be contributed to lack of communication. Increased life expectancy should bring with it the need for better communication skills.

As parents and spouses, we must implement and keep applying some of the suggestions and considerations mentioned on the last few pages. Even with this we may get very angry and discouraged as we help our kids grow. No society can survive without placing some limits on the behavior of its members (Dinkmeyer and McKay, 1976). We have to teach laws and values while we try to remove suspicion and promote trust. We must discipline to be sure, but in our attempts to be firm we must not lose sight of what is fair and what is actually effective.

I do believe there are those among us who are poor responders and cause problems because of our unawareness. While striving for the ideal of being simultaneously firm and open to feeling, influential and understanding, we must be able to see that we can never be perfect, but that we can be better. In our attempts to communicate we should understand that there is no such thing as a perfect responder or a perfect listener. We all have room for improvement and need to constantly assess our communication effectiveness. Let us look again at how we try to communicate. Remember, man is the only animal who can re-evaluate.

Business and Communication

Northwestern University's 32nd Endicott report, authored by retired director of placement, Frank Endicott, offered some basis to the idea that the skills being discussed in this book are needed in the business world. The report[3] reveals that employers want college grads with more practical experience *and* better communication skills. Endicott reports, "As the college graduate takes on the responsibility of a job, he or she must be able to deal with other employees and customers. It is almost impossible to be successful in business if your personality irritates or if you are unable to work cooperatively." An employer seemed to agree when he said, "Students should sharpen their communication skills because people spend half their corporate life communicating with each other.

In taking a second look at the Endicott report, it seemed to me that business was saying that personal communication skills, such as listening and responding, are very important. On the other hand, it seems that so much of what students learn in college must be read from a book, that when they begin learning their new work, listening and responding skills are not refined and it becomes difficult for business to help students with the transition from college. Add to this the probable "ordinary men" (Egan, 1975) in communication skills serving as executives for companies and we have an immediate source for complex, far-reaching communication problems within business and industry. And notice I said *within*. The communication skills I am focusing on in this book should take place everywhere. So what happens when people untrained in these skills, who have difficulty communicating within, have to perform *outside* for the business? To my way of thinking it is very costly to the business, both on the outside and on the inside.

I hope the following ideas will illustrate my position as to the need for better communication in business.

First of all, I think the days of the hard-sell, high-pressure techniques are numbered if not over. (Recall the example of the Hardsell Real Estate Co.) People want their needs met rather than the needs of some company or of a salesperson with whom they are talking. People are afraid, because of inflation, to part with their money. Salespeople, or those in business, must know how to show interest and establish rapport and credibility. It is difficult, if not impossible, to sell people anything if they don't trust you. Winning trust should be the first goal of anyone in business. But think about how most people view insurance salespeople, automobile salespeople, or those

[3] Excerpts reprinted courtesy of the *Chicago Tribune*. From an article by Carole A. Carmichael: Sunday Edition, Jan. 1, 1978.

selling appliances. Yes, there seems to be little allusion to feeling when cold, hard cash is at stake. Sales personnel can and should be taught to respond with more empathy and sensitivity. Many businesses could promote images far better than they have by training employees and management people to understand and then implement the skills suggested here.

LLPs don't just disappear in the business world! They are universal; so they have to affect business, and I think they do to a far greater extent than is currently realized. Often times businesses are aware of this communication problem, but have no idea how to correct it. The fact is that people in business can be taught these skills. Personnel directors should be trained in these techniques and prospective employees could be interviewed and tested to discover their facility (or lack of it) in interpersonal communication skills. Too many seminars are held on persuasion techniques or "how to sell your product" rather than on "how to listen" or "how to relate to your clients." More information than ever before is available about listening, responding, voice sound, body language, and attending to a person. And more people than ever before are aware of poor communication techniques. Business, then, could benefit from spending money on implementation of interpersonal communication systems that don't turn people off.

Of course, permanent implementation of such programs would be difficult and would involve continuous monitoring. Few people are trained to do this type of work. Turnover would cause the skills to have to be retaught to all new workers, although all new employees in *any* business should have some training in these skills. Many people would become defensive and anxious about having to make changes; nevertheless, I think the research indicates the necessity for such programs in business. I'm sure many business executives would agree with me. They know how serious it is when communication breaks down between two people, but when it breaks down with all company members, it is financially chaotic.

It seems safe to say that application of these skills can promote, at the very least, the understanding and therefore the possible solution to problems people within the organization may be encountering. On the other hand, when these skills are not implemented, employees will withdraw from the LLPs of their superiors because they think they are never heard and understood. This withdrawing in a business situation is no different than a child's withdrawing from his parents or a teacher. The "gap" is forever visible in business just as it is elsewhere. The vast majority of superiors break all of the rules. They advertise "My door is always open," but the way they respond says "The door is only ajar!" As a result, the company actually creates unhappy employees.

The "superiors," clinging to their LLPs, suppress enthusiasm and desire and have a great effect on the *future* energy of the employees. Surely, our LLPs play a very important role in the much publicized "productivity lag" in the United States. Workers withdraw their energy because they don't feel listened to. Their energy withdrawal can be correlated very highly with company costs, formulation of unions, and, yes, even strikes. Keep in mind that unions are caused, they just don't happen. People quit jobs because they feel their work is taken for granted. They do not feel appreciated. Being appreciated and recognized as being useful have to be basic needs in all humans. Plaques, dinners, certificates, gold watches, trips, and bonuses are just not enough to sustain psychological needs or to keep workers from withdrawing from poor communication techniques.

Withdrawing occurs often as a result of the power LLPs used by the majority of leaders. We learned in the last chapter that leaders incorporating the communication skills described in this book can influence people without using power (Gordon, 1977). As we have noted, not using power is the key to leader effectiveness (Gordon, 1977).

Leaders who choose coercive power as their system of leadership will find the results to be not very beneficial in terms of physical and mental health (Gordon, 1977, p. 257). A leadership style that is based on using power in communication will require the leader to maintain a rather consistent attitude of suspicion and distrust (Gordon, 1977, p. 257). And as Dr. Gordon so well stated:

> You'll have to be guarded in what you tell people, be on guard to detect signs of resistance to your power (or outright insubordination). Along with this vigilance, as an authoritarian leader you will find yourself viewing others as possessing limited capacity, and low potential for self-direction, for constructive change and personal development, for thinking for themselves (Gordon, 1977, p. 257).

What a price to pay for an ineffective communication system!

Leaders who play the power game are really saying, "Feelings don't belong here." Yet there is evidence that expressing feelings actually increases a group's effectiveness and productivity (Gordon, 1977, p. 77). Newspaper articles such as the one shown here are discovered often, as this one was in the *Chicago Tribune*. The articles offer some evidence as to the results of power and insensitive communication in business.

'Organizational' consultants delve into quality of work life

BALTIMORE (UPI)—Sometimes high salaries, plush offices, private parking, and free country club memberships do nothing to boost staff morale. That's when it can be smart to let your employes tell what bothers them.

"All you're doing is helping them spark off a discussion about things they don't usually talk about," said Allan Drexler, organizational consultant.

Drexler was hired by a Washington executive at $600 a day to conduct confidential staff interviews. He identified basic staff complaints that sapped morale and productivity. One complaint was that the company did not care about its employes.

The executive was dismayed, but hired the Annapolis, Md., consultant to implement a two-year program to build morale. It included discussion groups to help the staff find ways to improve attitudes and the work environment.

AN INCREASING number of corporate executives are using organizational consultants to improve the quality of life at work.

Organizational development specialists are not limited to diagnosing morale problems. Consultants lead training seminars, help devise organizational goals, and coach executives on how to combat stress.

Unions and management have hired the specialists after discovering that some issues cannot be settled at the bargaining table. More and more unionized factories—particularly in the automobile industry—are hiring organizational consultants to set up worker-management teams on productivity and employe morale.

"There is a limit to what collective bargaining can achieve for the worker," said Michael MacCoby, 47, a Washington-based consultant who has set up worker-management teams for several large manufacturers. MacCoby helped workers and managers set production goals at an automobile parts factory in Tennessee.

THE SAME PRINCIPLES are being applied by General Motors and the United Auto Workers to improve productivity and morale at a GM plant in Tarrytown, N.Y. Organizational consultants say they provide the objectivity only an outsider can bring to resolve staff conflict or help identify priorities.

"I see my role as asking the unaskable questions and raising the unthinkable issues because I don't have any stake in the outcome," said Elaine Lowery, 37, who specializes in consultant work to help nonprofit community organizations in Baltimore.

Not all requests for help result from a need to deal with a rebellious or unhappy staff.

Consultant Mary Sharer, of Reston, Va., said, "Some people are just interested in thinking about the future, about how their organizations might grow and expand. It might be an internal change to help us make that rearrangement more productive." Her clients have included Johnson and Johnson, Warner-Lambert, FMC and the United States Department of Transportation.

ORGANIZATIONAL DEVELOPMENT is rooted in the famous Hawthorne experiments of 1927 at Western Electric Co.'s plant in Cicero, Ill. Employes were subjected to carefully measured changes in work, hours, rest periods, and supervision to determine which factors affected job performance.

Researchers concluded that changed factors were less important in improving performance and morale than the employes' sense that someone was paying attention to them.

The field gained popularity in the early 1960s—about the time Drexler gave up a tenured professorship at the University of Cincinnati for full-time consulting.

He said the secret to organizational consulting is to win people's trust and make them think their personal well-being is as important as that of the organization.

"THE PEOPLE HAVE to learn that management is not trying to hustle them — this time," he said. "People really want to believe management is serious this time; they don't want to blow up the place. They don't want to live in all this misery."

Critics contend management uses organizational specialists to create the illusion employes are getting a better deal. Sharer said some managers decide not to change anything even after they are told what changes could be made.

MacCoby, who accepts work only in highly unionized plants, said his work differs from that of other consultants.

"THE DIFFERENCE BETWEEN the two approaches," he said, "is the organizational development person who works for management is concerned with improving efficiency and getting people to communicate better. But it all depends on the good faith of management. If management just decides it doesn't like it anymore, it can unilaterally stop things."

But Sharer said it is "not necessarily a bad thing" when executives ignore consultants' recommendations.

"We are there," she said, "to help the decision-making people to get the information so they can make more informed choices."

Reprinted by permission of United Press International

QWL is a term becoming popular in the business world. It means Quality of Work Life. This particular article points to the fact that "morale and productivity have been sapped," that the company "doesn't care about employees" and there is a need to get "people to communicate better" and "people should have a chance to talk about the things they don't usually talk about." Although the article does not mention LLPs as the possible culprit in this communication breakdown, you can deduce that they are present.

As the article suggests, there is a limit on what collective bargaining can achieve. The closing of the communication gap is seldom bargained for by either side. LLPs, used on both sides in collective bargaining, only cause the two groups to become more bitter, to move further apart. We might call it the "bargaining gap." Tangible items can be negotiated for, but "morale," "diminishing spirits," and "sapped productivity" aren't often among the items found on the agenda of negotiations meetings.

It happens time and time again in the bargaining process where money, fringe benefits, or other materialistic items are publicized as the "points of disagreement" or "still to be negotiated items." What has often happened is that negotiators have allowed LLPs to creep into the negotiating communication process. We must understand here that LLPs are often "putdowns," they are words uttered by a negotiator on one side or the other that attacks someone or the group on the opposing side "on a personal level." LLPs, subtle as they are, used by management cause unions to become "tighter," and LLPs used by union representatives cause management or the "company" to use more power. The human relations aspect is forgotten! Our democratic processes shouldn't involve this much conflict, but the ubiquitous LLPs often secretly destroy the negotiation process. The resentment process begins and makes negotiating very difficult.

The newspaper article just referred to mentioned the famous Hawthorne experiment where researchers concluded that changed factors were less important in improving performance and morale than the employees' sense that someone was paying attention to them. As a reader, do you find it disturbing to learn that the date of the Hawthorne study was 1927? It's been a long time since Babe Ruth hit sixty home runs (1927) and even now we *really* haven't tried to do much about the elimination of power LLPs in organizations. Yet, it seems to me, that LLPs are the real culprit researchers found to be contributing to the employees' sense that they were being neglected. It would seem, then, that LLPs were discovered in 1927, but have largely been ignored. Disregarding this research has cost companies and other organizations millions of dollars. Remember, unions don't just happen, they are caused, and at least part of the cause was discovered in 1927. However, "improper communication" by management wasn't identified as a *major* contributor to the cause. Unions flourish today because of the ignoring of this research, and they will continue to do so until programs are implemented to diminish the need for power to be a factor in organizations. We do have a *few* companies and organizations that do not have to have unions to "balance the power." Many are on the brink! Many executives are aware of "union talk," but are unaware that "company LLPs" are no doubt contributing to this talk. The executives are aware of the Hawthorne effect, *but not the LLP effect!*

Of course it is sad, unfortunate indeed, that the power differential even exists. Organizational leaders must understand that few people join an organization *wanting* to organize against it. The use of power by leaders nearly forces employees to "balance the power." We must understand that it is the communication process that contributes greatly to this need of "balancing power." Somehow we have got to implement the concept that feelings are not dangerous for a leader to deal with, but a friend they can count on to establish the proper environment for the organization to prosper (Gordon, 1977). Energy used for "union contracts" can be used elsewhere for the benefit of the organization.

Once again the point is that confrontations can be made with minimum use of power. Decisions can be made, and if feelings are handled properly, the decision may be accepted and implemented. Mandated decisions, no matter how small, can eventually cause unrest, especially if feelings are not alluded to. A phrase made familiar to me several years ago seems appropriate here: If two people are in business together and both of them think alike, one of them is not needed. So conflicts and disagreements will arise, but most disagreements can be brought to an amicable conclusion if the feelings from both sides are heard, not judged, but *heard,* or better still, listened to and responded to in a *sensitive* manner.

All of the signs point to the idea that leaders should be taught these skills before anyone else in an organization. If leaders can give up their LLPs, there will be less conflict because they are the ones called upon to resolve conflicts, not cause more. Just teaching managers, supervisors, department heads, or division leaders how to pick up feelings when an employee says something about himself or herself would be a good beginning. They, just as teachers and parents, can learn to not give those people working under their leadership "a wall to bounce their ball off of" (Lair, 1969). Inability to do this may cause these superiors to lose control. They may be in charge, but not in control. Control means things run smoothly and few people are concerned about who is in charge.

Conflicts often smolder in the ranks, and leaders can use the skills to settle disputes that are brought to them. At the very least they can make both sides feel as though they were treated equally. It seems safe to say that if a leader lingers in several of our categories more often with one person or group than another, that person or group will learn to withdraw, to question, to doubt, to distrust, and as we now know, will become discouraged. Discouraged workers are not effective workers. They may not be very productive. As we have said, it is no different than a student who believes "the teacher doesn't care." Both the student and the worker will develop a negative attitude toward their work.

Too many businesses and other groups are organized around the concept that administration makes the decisions, mandates them to employees for implementation, and waits for good results as a result of this mandate. This one-way communication is simply another way to say "power LLPs are at work." Employees feel rejected, their confidence suffers, they become discouraged and disillusioned, and they withdraw from the communication process. They often "rebel in very human ways by job hopping, absenteeism, apathetic attitudes, antagonism, and malicious mischief" (Gordon, 1977, p. 9). There is "preventative medicine" available if only more leaders would secure "a prescription."

Research has validated such "togetherness" needs for years, but business, as education, pays attention to research in the "hardware department" rather than in the "human relations" department. Better treads for tires, Computer-Assisted Instruction, break-proof glass, smaller transistors, audio-visual aids, pushbutton devices, and modular scheduling are all results of research that was paid attention to *now*. The research findings in human relations should, to many observers, be instituted *now,* but they aren't. It is easy to explain why! Those in organizations with power are uncomfortable in giving it up, and as we have learned "those in power defend their use of it on the grounds that it takes less time to solve conflicts" (Gordon, 1977, p. 166). We know better don't we? As Dr. Gordon implied in his informative book:

> Perhaps it is inevitable that coercive power generates the very forces that eventually will combat it and bring about a more equitable balance of power (Gordon, 1977, p. 165).

Coercive power is generated by our communication style. Leaders in organizations could earn respect, appreciation, and cooperation by improving their human relations techniques. The research is on their side, not against them, when they make this decision. Mistakes in human relations are becoming more costly to businesses than mistakes in production or advertising. These mistakes compound themselves. For example, because of economic conditions, many people can't afford to quit their jobs so they stay on, but production declines, morale suffers, and stress is very evident. In my view, the stress people may witness in exchanging their LLPs for more refined communication skills does not approach the intensity of stress most employees and executives encounter in our society's businesses. Money spent for a communication skills program would be better as a company investment than stocks are for most companies!

This brings me to an interesting phenomenon I see happening in our society. Many businesses are rapidly becoming popular by teaching business executives, managers, and employees relaxation techniques and by providing exercise programs designed to eliminate or prevent harmful stress. Thousands of dollars are spent annually on these programs.

I believe these programs are needed, but I think they could be more complete, more effective, if they included training in interpersonal communication skills. Stress is caused by worry, doubt, lack of trust, misunderstandings, and so forth. These common emotional states can be somewhat diminished by the better use of communication skills.

In looking at the executive who returns to work after a week-long seminar of learning relaxation and/or exercise techniques, we find the executive will still be facing the same old communication and relating problems. Techniques have been learned which only give the executive relief. This leader has not learned to listen and respond in such a way that can help eliminate or prevent stressful situations from arising. *We induce stress with our LLPs!* Interpersonal skills should, therefore, be looked upon as having the ability to prolong an executive's life nearly as much as stress eliminating techniques or exercise programs. Again, it seems to be a "Catch 22" because the executives are still not able to adequately deal with two major factors that cause stress . . . their LLPs and the LLPs of others.

So very often stressful times occur for executives, and these uneasy times are prolonged because of the executive's inability to listen and respond effectively to company clients or to people who work under his or her leadership. A high level of understanding simply does not exist in these companies. Just take a look at our seven rules and categories and see how often they are broken in the business world. Look again at the categories mentioned in the last chapter. Do executives and sales representatives whom you know or with whom you have come in contact fit into any of these categories? Of course they do, because most of them have to be "ordinary men" (Egan, 1975) in communication skills, just like the rest of us. I realize persuasion techniques, use of logic, and information gathering through the use of questions, are all important in the business world, but they are overused in business just as in other areas in our society.

It is not difficult to identify two major problems in business or to see the direct link to interpersonal communications. Of course one is the inability to get along with people. The other is motivation of employees. A great deal has been said in this book about how to relate better, and the business leaders are well advised to incorporate these relating skills so they may establish better relationships and thereby overcome many motivational problems. Working people are motivated the same way students are in the schools . . . by being understood!

We added an R to the three Rs in education and we can do the same in business. Responsibility, recognition, and reward seem to be three very well accepted Rs in business. The R for relating should be added to business also.

BANVILLE, THOMAS G. *How to Listen—How to Be Heard.* Chicago: Nelson-Hall, 1978.

CARKHUFF, ROBERT R. and BERENSON, BERNARD G. *Beyond Counseling and Therapy.* New York: Holt, Rinehart and Winston, Inc., 1967.

DINKMEYER, DON and McKAY, GARY D. *Systematic Training for Effective Parenting: Parents Handbook,* Circle Pines, Minnesota: American Guidance Service, Inc., 1976.

DREIKURS, RUDOLF and CASSEL, PEARL. *Discipline Without Tears.* New York: Hawthorn Book, Inc., 1972. (Now Hawthorn/Dutton)

EGAN, G. *The Skilled Helper.* Monterey, California; Brooks/Cole Publishing Company, 1975.

GALLUP, GEORGE. Tenth Annual Gallup Poll of the Public's Attitude Toward Public Schools. *American Educator,* Winter, 1978, p. 5.

GORDON, THOMAS. *L.E.T. Leader Effectiveness Training.* Reprinted with permission of Wyden Books from *L.E.T. Leader Effectiveness Training* by Dr. Thomas Gordon. Copyright © 1977 by Dr. Thomas Gordon.

GROSS, MARTIN. *The Psychological Society.* New York: Random House, Inc., 1978.

LAIR, JESS. *"I Ain't Much Baby—But I'm All I've Got.* New York: Fawcett Publications, Inc. 1969, 1972. (Doubleday and Company)

LILLIBRIDGE, MICHAEL E. and KLUKKEN, GARY. Interpersonal Communication Skills, Cassette Tape Series, Affective House, Tulsa, Oklahoma, 1977.

POWELL, JOHN S. J. *Why Am I Afraid to Tell You Who I Am?.* Niles, Illinois: Argus Communications. © 1969.

SHERTZER, B. and STONE, S. *Fundamentals of Guidance.* Boston: Houghton-Mifflin Co., 1976.

six

How to Use This Book

Upon finishing the first five chapters in this book, the reader who recognizes a need to change communication skills will see a need to keep the book handy. It is doubtful that communications can be improved by merely reading the book. Those wanting to learn the skills described in these pages will need to refer to the book often, so try and keep it accessible.

To achieve the desired change, readers should practice, practice, practice. But, as in the development of most skills, they must be practiced the correct way in order to be perfected.

First, we can come to realize the difference between a conversation and a more personal communication. Since we have read and now understand the ideas in the first five chapters, I am hopeful the difference has become clear. To review and simplify, let's say the difference is "idle chatter" or an "informal interchange" as compared to "talk involving feeling."

You can begin using the book by first simply listening to people talk and responding to them. Then shortly after the communication process is completed, spend a few minutes with the book in hand. At this time you should try to evaluate whether or not you listened and responded appropriately. I suggest asking yourself, "How *costly* is what I just said in terms of this relationship?" All conversations are either good or bad. As has been pointed out, it takes a great deal of skill just to remain neutral and not be harmful. So it becomes imperative that we practice and recognize when we are making "costly" remarks.

Of course, "costly" remarks are those words we utter during the relationship gap without first listening for feeling. These are the remarks we make that too often break our rules; or they are comments that prevent us from eliminating obstacles of poor communication, and, unknowingly, cause us to categorize ourselves as poor communicators. Noncostly remarks are good remarks which foster good relationships. No "cost" in responding is a goal for which we can strive.

Obviously, we can "cost" ourselves a great deal in the way we listen. We can start now in checking for "the things we really listen for" by referring to the book after talking with someone. We can ask ourselves things like, "There seemed to be some feeling in what the person said to me. Did I relate to the feeling or did I miss it?" I would strongly urge readers to turn to the list of feeling words on page 14 and refer to it often. First, figure out if what a person said seemed to relate a pleasant or unpleasant feeling. Then go down the list under the proper heading and see which word or words best describe the feeling heard. We will discover that we can usually find a better word than the one we used or even one we were thinking of using. Once the word has been located, we should ask ourselves, "Did I actually hear that specific feeling and did I come close to responding to it?"

For example, did we minimize feeling? Did we allow logic to get in the way? Were we sending a solution? Did we assume too much? Just what was "costly?" Possibly it was just a friendly interchange with "no harm, no foul." If we didn't respond to feeling, we can discover a clue as to why we didn't by checking at the top of the pages in the book.

The book is not cumbersome. It is designed to allow you to thumb through rather quickly and check valuable clues. Because this process is quick and uncomplicated, you can afford yourself the opportunity to improve your communication techniques. Try to discover how to prevent a "costly" future response. It may be necessary to re-read pages on which certain helpful clues are found.

By checking through the book after many conversations with

people, we will discover what "categories" we usually find ourselves in, or what "obstacles" are getting in the way of our responding better. No doubt pet remarks will be uncovered which have been "costly" to us in the past.

Egan (1975) alluded to "psychological presence," so we might ask, "What can we do to improve the quality of our presence?" It is a worthwhile question to ask ourselves. Often the thing we can do is pause or take a little more time to think about what may be costly before we respond. It may be that we send a quick solution or have advice for everybody. Or, are we starting responses with, "You should" or "Why don't you try . . . ? Are we encouraging or are we ridiculing? Do we often accept feelings or are we nonaccepting or judgmental? Do we respond to people in such a way that they are made to feel unable to do things? Do we express to much sympathy or praise when we could be focusing on feelings? Are we questioning or probing and missing the point? By systematically checking in the book, we can begin to identify those "costly" habits (LLPs) ingrained within us and rid ourselves of them.

We should also consider the fact that we hear ourselves more than anyone else hears us. We are, therefore, responsible for changing ourselves since we are, with the aid of the techniques suggested, more able to identify what changes are needed. We can do it!

Another checkpoint worth consideration is one mentioned by Carkhuff and Berenson. They suggested that we might ask ourselves, "Is what I just said too far removed emotionally from the person's feelings?"[1] As persons with LLPs our responses are too often far removed from the other person's emotions to help eliminate any threat to the relationship. We can use the book to develop a program which will improve our communications instead of constantly handing out costly prescriptions, agendas, and programs for those around us.

To efficiently use this book, it seems worthwhile to recall that we spend most of our time thinking about ourselves. This costly exercise makes it twice as difficult to remove ourselves from the life of another person at the times we should. In regard to this, Benjamin suggested that we consider whether or not "we are doing it to some-

---

[1] From *BEYOND COUNSELING AND THERAPY* by Robert R. Carkhuff and Bernard G. Berenson. Copyright © 1967 by Holt, Rinehart and Winston, Inc. Reprinted by permission of Holt, Rinehart and Winston.

one or with someone" (Benjamin, 1969, p. 96). Do we respond so people will want to take something from us, or do we respond so they feel we are injecting something into them?

All of these suggestions are attempts to assist us in analyzing the many conversations we have each day of our lives. Conscientious use of the book should afford us the opportunity to experience ourselves and recognize changes that we would like to make in our communications.

Use the book to check back on the day's conversations. Study the improvements you have made and what you seemed to have done that might have been "costly." Also, during the course of a day, listen to conversations in which you are not involved. Remember (or jot down somewhere) errors heard and, when it is convenient, use the book to look up corrections. Often, you will hear an error, but will not be sure exactly what the error is. It may help you improve to refer to the book and figure out what error was made.

Another way to practice is to watch TV and evaluate the communication process taking place between the people talking on the programs. Try to think of the feeling level and what you would say in response to the comments made in the TV programs. Soap operas are great for this as well as medical programs and movies with an emotional theme.

The book can be used in a multitude of ways. Work with different ideas until improvements are seen. For example, if you express some fear, joy, or discouragement to a friend, take note as to how you feel and how your friend responds to your feelings. What rules did the friend break? What obstacles seem to be blocking your friend? In which categories does he seem to be placing himself? (Be careful here because your friend is not the one practicing these better techniques of communication. It is very easy to become too critical of others once these skills are well incorporated into our communication systems.) After talking with your friend, check through the book to see how your friend could have made a better response to your feelings. In my view using your own feelings is one of the best ways to practice and become more familiar with obstacles to good communication.

To use the book in another way, encourage someone you know well and are often with, to read the book and then practice together. Write down examples of conversations that have feeling involved in them. These ideas can come from television, newspapers, movies, magazine articles, and novels, as well as everyday conversations. Make a response to these conversations and then use the book to check each other as to the appropriateness of the responses. This does not take a great deal of time and is an excellent way to practice. (Some examples are included near the end of this chapter.)

Other communication difficulties that use of the book can help eliminate, or at least minimize, are as follows: By checking our communication patterns, we can tell if we are really communicating or just biding our time until the problem goes away. We can soon discover whether or not we really communicate the idea that the other person's viewpoint is important. We can observe if we come on as a superior person, who usually has answers for people. We can begin to understand if our words often cause stress or relieve it. If we do some of these costly things on a regular basis, it would no doubt benefit us to diminish this trait by becoming more familiar with the obstacles, categories, rules, starters, and feeling word list.

No doubt the attitudes, ideas, feelings, and prejudices we previously held about people will be challenged if we choose to use this book frequently. The suggestions made are not meant to dominate anyone's life. There is no intent to promote any guilt or insecurity, but a different attitude about people must develop within readers if constructive changes in communication are to be made.

Be aware also that we have to let our feelings, ideas, values, and attitudes be known in order to be real and empathetic. One of the best ways I know to become depressed is to store up a lot of feeling. Expressing these ideas, feelings, values, and attitudes often approaches the confronting stage, but as Carkhuff and Berenson mentioned, "A life without confrontation is directionless, passive and impotent"[2] (Carkhuff and Berenson, 1967, p. 172). Judgment is the keynote. I often equate it to learning to parallel park an automobile. We can practice with some rules and develop judgment, and the skill and confidence eventually become part of us.

We will know we have mastered this judgment when we are calm and peaceful before we respond. We should notice a difference in the content of our responses and notice that our LLPs are not

---

[2] From *BEYOND COUNSELING AND THERAPY* by Robert R. Carkhuff and Bernard G. Berenson. Copyright © 1967 by Holt, Rinehart and Winston, Inc. Reprinted by permission of Holt, Rinehart and Winston.

present as often . . . Our LLPs will, however, always be with us; the purpose of this book is to help us recognize and diffuse them as much as possible. We *can* study ourselves and overcome shortcomings which our LLPs have gradually developed within all of us.

It may also be helpful to become very familiar with the definition of the "relationship gap." Think of the gap time we know we have and ask, "Was I thinking about what I was going to say, or was I listening and trying to experience what the person was feeling?" Ask, "Did I use the gap time wisely?" If you don't think you used it very well, check in the book to see what could have been done to improve the use of the gap time.

Included in this chapter are several examples of "costly" remarks in interpersonal communication. It is hoped these examples will give readers ideas as to how to use this book. Most of the examples used are taken from real life situations. Many were arrived at as I listened to people around me respond to events instead of feeling. Some are fictitious, but based on real-life situations. Many came to me as I was using the material mentioned in this book to try and improve my counseling skills and communication with my friends, family, and business associates.

The examples are organized so that a brief explanation is given as to the event and what someone said in regard to that event. A costly response is shown to readers and a less costly response is suggested. A general critique or suggestion for applying the material in the book is often included for the reader. Feeling words, usually left out of costly responses, are underlined in the suggested responses. Of course, the reasons behind each suggested response can be found in the book. There are no right or wrong answers, but there are better ones than those first given.

Examples

1.   A high school boy says to his coach, "I'm not sure I'm going to be here next year to play on the golf team. My parents have separated. My Dad lives in another school district. I don't know what to do . . . I like it in this school and I have a lot of friends here."

Costly response: "You will have to make that decision. It is a difficult situation. Of course, we would like for you to stay here, but you have to do what is right for you."

Suggested response: "Sounds as though you are <u>torn</u> and somewhat <u>confused</u> as to what steps to take."

Critique: Check the word list for feeling words. The coach did not relate to the boy's feelings (torn and confused). The word list will provide more feeling words that might apply to this example.

The coach tried to persuade a little when he said, "We would like." I can't prove it, but I think the boy is more likely to stay with the coach if his feelings are picked up than if he feels somewhat coerced and not listened to. Adding pressure to the boy's decision will not help the relationship. The coach related to the obvious (an event) instead of feeling. Some evaluation and opinion were interjected, several rules were broken. In this case rules 1, 2, 5, and 7 were broken. (To practice using the book check and see which rules are broken in each example). Notice that "Sounds as though . . ." is a starter and use of it makes it easier to get at the feeling level.

2.   A ten year old was spending some quiet time with her mother. The mother was recently divorced and the father was no longer living in the house. The young girl said, "I love you Mom, but I don't like it when I come home and I only have a Mom, and not a Dad to talk with."

Costly response: "I don't like it either, but you know you can't have both right now. Come on now, try to cheer up."

Suggested response: "It's as though you feel somewhat <u>lost</u> without Daddy and it makes you <u>unhappy</u>."

Critique: In the costly remark an attempt is made to persuade the feelings to go away. It is difficult to say the right thing in a situation such as this, but a poor response just makes the relationship suffer a bit. It is difficult in a moment such as this, and we often respond out of panic because we simply can't deal with the situation. We want it to end as soon as possible. It is better, in building relationships, to try and deal with these difficult moments.

Minimizing is certainly present here. The mother started her response with "I" which often gets us in trouble. "You feel" is a better way to start and I suggest readers use it often when just beginning this new process of communication. Is the mother conveying the idea that she heard her daughter's feeling?

3.   This is an example (alluded to in Chapter II) of how improper responding in business can send a relationship reeling. A middle-aged couple, seeking to buy a house, have just completed a tour of a house with a real estate agent. The middle-aged lady says to the real estate agent, "We like the house very much, but I'm afraid my father can't combat the stairs. He has arthritis and will be living here with us most of the time."

Costly response: "There is a bath and a bedroom downstairs. Perhaps he wouldn't have to go upstairs very often."

Suggested response: "You are really <u>concerned</u> about how well a house will meet your father's needs."

Critique: Try this critique yourself. See if you can now write down some of the errors made in this communication process. You should be able to identify the rules broken and place the real estate agent in several "categories."

4.   A nurse enters the room of a hospital patient. The patient says, "This food is lousy! It's not fit for a dog! I'm starving to death."

Costly response: "I eat it every day. We don't get many complaints. You need to eat to get stronger." (Most nurses don't respond this way, but some do after they get to know a patient and they allow their LLPs to slip back into the communication system).

Suggested response: "It's as if you are <u>at the mercy of</u> this place." Or, "It's <u>disgusting</u> to not get something you like to eat when you are so hungry."

Critique: There may not be an easy way to handle this situation, particularly if the patient is under doctor orders to maintain a strict diet, but compare the costly response and the suggested response. The less rules we break the better off we will be in relating to this person. "I eat it everyday" is the beginning of persuasion and use of logic to get the patient to feel better. "We don't get many complaints" is an attempt to use logic and an attempt to explain feelings away by assuming that the taste of all patients is universal. The theme the nurse is projecting is that if the majority of people feel a certain way, this patient should also feel the same. It isn't effective! Will the person feel listened to?

5.   A friend says to you, "I'm going into the hospital tomorrow. I have been on some kind of medication. The doctor said he wants to check me over. Something about my liver . . . I don't know . . . I don't know what is going on. He doesn't tell me much."

Costly response: "What doctor do you go to?" Or, "What hospital will you be in?"

Suggested response: "I get the impression you are a little apprehensive because you aren't sure what is wrong." Or, "You sound somewhat apprehensive."

Critique: "What doctor do you go to," is a statement far removed from how the person is feeling. It shows curiosity. What are we going to say when we find out who the doctor is? This is a good example as to how questions can lead us into trouble in communicating. When we ask questions we should become aware of what they do to the communication process. If this is a bothersome area for you, I suggest you re-read the pages on questions. A simple question like, "What doctor do you go to?" can start widening the relationship gap ever so slightly. Suppose the person says, "I go to Dr. Highpockets." If we aren't careful, we make matters worse by saying something like, "My sister went to him with a liver problem and was in the hospital for a month." The first response didn't seem so damaging, but it moved us so far from what the person was expressing in the way of feeling that it at least started the damage. Most people do not want to hear words that make them feel worse, but we can and do make them feel worse by missing feeling, asking a question, and allowing an ingrained response to slip in before we are aware of what we have done.

6.   A thirteen-year-old girl says to her father, "Dad, should I go to Notre Dame or Ole Miss?"

Costly response: "It's a little early to be applying to a college. Don't be worrying yourself about those things now." Or, "You will have to decide many things like: Do you want to be close to home? What are you going to major in? What does it cost to go to Notre Dame as compared to Ole Miss?"

Suggested response: You seem to be wondering about where you might go to school." (Allow her to pursue more if she wants to do so).

Critique: In this case, responding to feeling removes the urge to analyze the situation and figure out how important it seems to be to each of us. The other person (the daughter) has to figure out how important it is to dwell on this subject. This is not for us to decide. Here is another example of an individual responding to an event (going to college) rather than his daughter's feelings (wondering). Of course, finances, a major, location of the school, and other considerations will eventually need to be discussed, but the father may be "beyond" his daughter in discussing these items now.

7. As is often the case, a high school student becomes very hostile toward his parents because they will not allow him to do something he really wants to do. He is discussing the problem with a teacher and says, "What is their problem? How do they know what is best for me?"

Costly response: "They are just trying to help you. I'm sure they don't want to see you make a bad decision."

Suggested response: "I get the impression you feel <u>bitter</u> about their decision."

Critique: You try this one. Check the rules broken and then thumb through the tops of the pages and see how many errors you can identify. Can you find other feeling words that seem appropriate?

8. In this situation a young girl could be talking to a teacher, parent, counselor, or neighbor. The girls says, "My friend cheated on a test and I gave her some of the answers. I feel like I should report the incident, but it will cause both of us problems."

Costly response: "That's a tough one. Honesty is usually the best policy. Can't you two work out what to do?"

Suggested response: "Guess you're feeling <u>trapped</u> and having trouble deciding what to do."

Critique: "That's a tough one," begins to analyze the situation. It is tough, but it doesn't do much good to tell a person it is tough unless *they* say it first. "Honesty is the best policy," is a judgment and an opinion coming from the responder's value system. It is an attempt to solve the problem for the person. It serves to persuade the person to take some action. "Can't the two of you work out what to do?" is the use of logic and assumes a great deal. It also says to the person "I am not even willing to listen, so go away and work out the problem." We can listen and *help* an individual make a decision without making it for him or her and without making him or her dependent on us. In this example the confidant is participating in the process of making this person dependent on other people to make difficult decisions. He coaxes the person to go away by saying, "Can't the two of you" and strongly suggests that honesty is the best policy. He has sent a "magical solution." It really becomes confusing to a person when we suggest, "You are dependent on me, but quickly take what I am giving you and solve this problem so I won't have to waste my time on it." It is simply better to listen and respond in such a way that the person is the one who makes the decisions.

9.   A teenager says to a friend, "I've really got it going! I made an A in English today and yesterday I found out I made the basketball team. Then today, my folks told me we are going to make a trip to Hawaii this summer. Do you believe all of this?"

Costly response: "Things are coming up roses," or worse "The last time I was in Hawaii it rained for a week." Or we often say, "Hey, neat! Send me a card."

Suggested response: "Yes, you really seem <u>proud</u> and <u>excited</u> about all of this."

Critique: Now I realize not all of the responses are harmful, but let's look at what happened. The costly response forgets about the A in English and making the basketball team. We often hear only the last part of what someone says to us. This person is not only proud, but also excited, and a response made to cover all feelings should include words from the list that seem to perform this function.

"You are not only proud, but excited," is a fine response if the voice tone is adequate. Keep in mind pleasant feelings, such as the ones being expressed here, are sometimes more difficult to handle than unpleasant feelings. We all know the exciting time will end before long, but we can respond in such a way that we don't have to be involved in its ending.

Consider the idea that people often ask questions without really wanting an answer. They want their feelings heard. "Do you believe all of this?" is an example of this type question.

10.   A friend says to you, "I may have to drop the night class I'm taking. I'm having to help out around the house more and more because my Dad is in the hospital. He is going to have major surgery. Mom is with him most of the time and I have to take care of the kids and do the housework. I can't seem to get any studying done."

Costly response: "That's too bad. What's wrong with your Dad?"

Suggested response: "Sounds as though you are <u>overwhelmed</u> with a lot happening at once."

Critique: You may be close enough to someone to feel comfortable in asking, "What is wrong with your Dad?" and I do not think this is terribly harmful. However, I think it is better to first pick up your friend's feelings about his class and his father and then possibly ask about details. Again, curiosity about, rather than interest in, someone comes out and in certain situations this can cause problems.

In this example, look up what categories we could place the costly response in. Also, check other feeling words that seem to apply to the situation. Try to find words that seem to describe the primary feeling.

11.   One friend says to another while they are discussing business, "You would not believe what is happening in our office. I'll sure be glad when it is over."

Costly response: "What is the problem? Are the bosses starting that reorganization talk again?"

Suggested response: "Sounds like you are feeling <u>edgy</u> about the whole thing." Or, "You sound like you are little <u>uneasy</u> about what is going on."

Critique: Try to avoid getting ahead of the speaker. How can we be sure someone wants to continue telling us about what is happening in the office? We can't! This is just another reason why it is usually best to go with the feeling just heard and allow the individual to determine if he wants to volunteer any more information. It is a fact in personal communication that a person listened to will reveal more than one questioned, probed, or persuaded to tell more.

In this situation, if the friend recognizes he is edgy, apprehensive, or uneasy he may choose to talk more about it. If we missed the feeling level of our friend, he may choose to clarify it for us, talk more about it, or just drop it, and all of these choices should be his and not ours.

12.   A student says to a teacher, "I don't have any friends in this class. I can't do my work."

Costly response: "Oh, I'm sure someone in here likes you. We all have feelings like that once in awhile."

Suggested response: "I get the impression you are feeling <u>neglected</u> and it is affecting your school work."

Critique: In my view the costly response is very harmful. It breaks rules 1, 2, 4, 6, and 7 and places us in several categories. So many exchanges with students are of a short duration that teachers should have little fear of having to make very many noncostly responses in succession. In this case, "We all" is a generalization. It minimizes feelings. Seldom is it beneficial to attempt to *universalize* feelings. There is a great deal of feeling being expressed in this classroom situation and the feeling should be responded to instead of using logic and an assumption that, "Someone in here likes you." Are teachers going to get into a verbal war of proving to a student that at least one person in the class truly likes him or her? If we assume things that we might have trouble documenting, we are probably headed for trouble in communicating to anyone. This is just another example of how we cover up our inability to help someone. If we don't have some sure-fire method of solving problems, we had better get back to responding to feeling instead of getting into something we can't handle.

13.   A playground supervisor or gym teacher has a child say, "They always choose me last! I know I'm not very good, but I do like to play. They never let me! What can I do?"

Costly response: "Ask them if you can do the choosing."

Suggested response: "It's like you're being <u>overlooked</u> and are having trouble figuring out what to do."

Critique: The supervisor may have to eventually help work out some plan in order for the child to be chosen. Remember, however, that we are trying to help people rely on their own strengths and not on ours. The suggested response lets the child know right away that his attempt to be heard is not in vain. The group is not hearing him, so it is nice for the child that someone is. It is tempting to answer the child's last question, "What can I do?" But we can't develop independence if we *always* answer this type question. We can learn to avoid this trap and train ourselves to respond to feeling. The costly response mentioned here sends a solution, uses logic, and minimizes feeling. Children use this type of question to apply pressure to adults to solve their problems. We must solve some problems, but we should not give in to this pressure as much as most adults do. Many fear the young people will begin to feel as though we don't care about them if we don't solve their problems for them. We need to cut back on the percentage of problems solved for our young people. Judgment as to *when* to give in is the key to fostering independence. For example, if the child in this example says (after our suggested response) that he is going "to hit somebody in the mouth," it might be best for us to intervene. If, however, the child says, "I'll get in somehow, it has happened before," then I think we can take a small risk and see if he or she can work it out.

14.   A man shopping for an advertised item is getting the runaround by several clerks in a department store. Finally, he says to a different clerk, "I've been to automotive, electronics, and sporting goods. I feel as though I'm in a revolving door! What the heck is going on here? Just tell me where I can buy this thing!"

Costly response: "We just hired a new manager and things are really up for grabs." Or, "I just started today."

Suggested response: "It sure sounds like you are getting the runaround. I'll try to help you."

Critique: To paraphrase and let a person know he or she is being heard can prevent or diffuse many explosive situations. "I just started today," does not come from the shopper's viewpoint and totally minimizes feelings. This clerk responded to the event, not the feeling. Look up other feeling words *after* you think of a few that might be applied in this example.

15.   A man who was recently employed by a large insurance company casually says to his boss, "Some of the guys in my part of the office sure don't seem very friendly. One of them said the way I dress wouldn't help me sell much insurance."

Costly response: "Just ignore them." (A popular response)

Suggested response: "Sounds like you are <u>disenchanted</u> with some of the guys working around you."

Critique: At least we know, "Just ignore them," is not a good response and breaks most of our rules. A father in one of my classes mentioned that he made such a response in a similar situation. He told the class that he knew immediately he had made an error in communication. He became a "solutioner" or an "advicer." The father said he knew the man needed someone to listen to him, but he chased him away with, "Just ignore them." He missed the discontent or disenchantment the new employee was expressing. We tend to do this frequently.

16.   A neighbor says to you, "My mother is really starting to get to me. You know my wife has been gone for close to two years now. Both of the kids are in college downstate, and I'd like to get out of the house more. She just insists that I stay with her almost every minute. I don't have a life of my own."

Costly response: "Better let her know how you feel. It is no picnic having someone control your life like that. I know, my aunt used to be that way." Or, "Well, you know, your Mom is nearly eighty and she probably needs you. You do so much for her."

Suggested response: "It's almost as though you are feeling <u>suffocated</u>." Or, "You feel as though you are being <u>intimidated</u> or something." Or, "Somehow it feels like you are being <u>hemmed in</u>."

Critique: The costly response offers advice, gives an opinion, sends a possible solution, and misuses logic. We must consider what might happen if our advice doesn't work or makes things worse. If we make things worse, what will we have for our neighbor next time he or she comes around?

People usually take action on feelings that they have become completely aware of, so it seems important to help them understand their feelings.

17.   Respond, as a supervisor, to this machine operator who has been operating an office machine for ten years. With the introduction of new electronic equipment the operator says, "I've been using this machine for X number of years. I like it and the work gets done. I'm doing just fine the way I am right now. I've used the new equipment and it just slows me down."

Costly response: "This new equipment will save us time and, therefore, will save us money. Use it for awhile and see if you don't like it."

Suggested response: In order to let the employee know he or she was heard, we might say something like, "Guess you are saying you are pretty comfortable with the old equipment and are <u>skeptical</u> of what the new equipment can do." The costly response, or something similar, may have to be said eventually, but when we have a choice to listen or try to push something down someone's throat, we better try the listening first. Persuasion, logic, and "missing feeling" are all present in the costly response. Persuasion is often necessary, but people usually change behavior when they want to and not when we want them to. People become more manageable when we attempt to gain their cooperation rather than just tell them what to do.

18.   A high school student says to his Dad, "Man, am I getting the shaft in Miss Crabbie's class. She hates my guts! No matter what happens in her class, it is my fault. If she doesn't get off my case soon, I'm going to blow my top!"

Costly response: "That will probably make things worse. There has to be a better way." Or, "What are you doing to upset her?" Or, "You are going to get some nutty teachers once in a while and you just have to learn to put up with it." Or, "Sounds to me like you had better talk to her about this."

Suggested response: "It's like you are <u>branded</u> and are feeling <u>intimidated</u>." Or, "What you are saying is you feel <u>picked on</u> and are at wits end to do anything about it."

Critique: Persuading the boy to calm down may help the situation, but we should also relate to the feeling being expressed. Just allowing a person to talk out a problem can be helpful. I see these attempts to "talk it out," but people get themselves in the way so much that the person with the problem can't do much to get his or her feelings out. We might also keep in mind that our solutions might not have as permanent an effect as those made by the people directly involved in the problem. Yet we may have to say, "I encourage you to work it out, but if it does become too difficult to handle, I'll be available for help."

19.   Here is an example of how interpersonal communication skills can be used in business. An angry woman calls the telephone company and says, "I just moved to this crazy town and I was told my phone would be hooked up yesterday. It is now 3:30 and after all of this waiting, I have not seen anyone from the phone company. Am I ever going to get my phone?"

Costly response: "Yes, you will get a phone. I'll run a check on it right away and see what happened."

Suggested response: "Sounds as though you have been rather patient. It is <u>irritating</u> when an appointment is broken. Sorry for the inconvenience, I'll check it out for you right now."

Critique: People in business often try to defend the business or apologize *first.* An apology may be in order, but responding to the customer's feeling about the business helps to establish credibility. This is often overlooked, and when the customer senses that his feelings are overlooked, he or she will continue to be upset . . . and possibly take his business to another company!

20.   On a break one CPA says to another, "I'm getting run down; twenty years of this is getting to me. I think I need a job change. It gets old working on the same old stuff all of the time."

Costly response: "I feel the same way you do. It does get to you; but what other field does our training fit into?"

Suggested response: "Somehow, after all of these years, it feels <u>discouraging</u> to you and you start <u>wondering</u> what else you can <u>do</u>."

Critique: Does misery love company? We can never be sure how intense someone's feeling is. I sometimes think our society teaches us to make the other person think we are miserable, and we think this will make him feel better. I think we are more apt to help a person feel better if the person's feelings are understood. Perhaps we overuse sympathy because it is a substitute for our usual lack of skill in dealing with problems. The costly response mentioned here probably won't change or damage this friendship very much, but it does show again how we quickly move from the emotions of a person to our own emotions or to an event.

Obviously, a few of these examples presented so far indicate more harm in personal communication than others. I have tried to present a wide range of emotion in these examples so people can look at and determine at what level of feeling they would like to make changes in their communication techniques. Possibly some readers need to improve responses when they hear pleasant feelings or very deep feelings.

Let's change the format somewhat and allow you, the reader, to participate in the critique. In the following examples you are encouraged to first read the statement someone makes and then read the response to it. After reading the response fill in (on the lines provided) the rules broken, the "categories" the responder places himself in, and then write in what feeling is missing from the response. (See example 1.)

Examples

1. A fellow worker says to you, "I'll tell you, I'm feeling a lot of pressure from my department head. He seems to play favorites. It's like I do as good a job as anyone else in the department and my work is never noticed. I'm about ready to ask for a transfer."

Response: "I'm sure he is not playing favorites. He has been one of our best leaders for over twenty years. Are you sure you aren't over reacting?"

What rules are broken?   1, 2, 3, 4, 5 and 7.

What categories does the responder place himself in?   Some are: Questioner, solutioner, advicer, minimizer, assumptionist.

What is the feeling being missed (expressed)?   neglect, degraded, discouraged, hurt, jilted, mistreated, ostracized, unsatisfied

Write in your response   Sounds as though you feel you are being neglected.

1. Take the feeling/not the event.
2. Use a feeling word. Don't minimize feelings.
3. Eliminate questions!
4. Eliminate logic and assumptions.
5. Don't send solutions or give advice.
6. Allow them to do the talking.
7. Eliminate evaluations, opinions, judgments, and analysis.

2. "I have been very nervous lately. It's scary! My husband passed away and I get uptight being in that big house all alone. Do you think I should sell it? I like the neighborhood and can't imagine where I would move to."

Response: "I can't tell you much about the housing market. I know they aren't selling so well right now."

What rules are broken? ____________________________

What categories does the responder place himself in? ________

____

What is the feeling being missed (expressed)? ______________

____

Write in your response ____________________________

____

____

____

3.   An assistant principal or dean says to a high school student, "I thought you were going to get your classes all set and start attending class." The student says, "I haven't been able to get in and see my counselor. I can't go to class until I get my schedule from her."

Response: "You know school started over a week ago. You better get in class."

What rules are broken? ____________________________

What categories does the responder place himself in? ________

____

What is the feeling being missed (expressed)? ______________

____

Write in your response ____________________________

____

____

____

4. "I can't wait until school starts. Working for my Dad is a pain. Just being around my Mom and Dad makes me feel like I'm under the control of some dictator. School is not so great, but it's better than being home."

Response: "Are you going back to State U. again?"

What rules are broken? _______________________________

What categories does the responder place himself in? ________

____

What is the feeling being missed (expressed)? ____________

____

Write in your response _________________________________

____

____

____

5. "I'm beginning to wonder if this job is worth it. In fact, I'm wondering about a lot of things lately. I'm not sure I love my wife and kids. I would like to be just like you and never be down and have to think about crazy things."

Response: "You have probably been working too hard. I get down once in a while, everyone does. It's human nature. Possibly you need to take some time off."

What rules are broken? _______________________________

What categories does the responder place himself in? ________

____

What is the feeling being missed (expressed)? ____________

____

Write in your response _________________________________

____

____

6. "I'm telling you this productivity push is too much for people on the assembly line to handle. They are tired all of the time and complain more than ever. I have been taking a lot of verbal abuse over it."

Response: "It has worked before and we haven't had many complaints in our other plants. It will blow over. Don't worry about it."

What rules are broken? ____

What categories does the responder place himself in? ________

____

What is the feeling being missed (expressed)? ________________

____

Write in your response ____

____

____

____

7. "I just think no one was listening in that last meeting. I know they weren't listening to me. It seems my ideas are never heard or used. Decisions are made every day, but there isn't the slightest bit of me in them."

Response: "Well, advertising is a tough business. Someone has to make the decisions."

What rules are broken? ____

What categories does the responder place himself in? ________

____

What is the feeling being missed (expressed)? ________________

____

Write in your response ____

____

____

____

8.   "I sold three policies today! It's a new record for me. I've been working so hard and it finally paid off!"

Response: "My record is three policies . . . I sold them before noon and played golf the rest of the day."

What rules are broken? ____

What categories does the responder place himself in? _________

____

What is the feeling being missed (expressed)? ________________

____

Write in your response ____

____

____

____

9.   A student says to a teacher or a counselor, "I can't go on like this! I have this bad ulcer. It keeps flaring up and I can't do my work. I'm on some kind of medication and it helps some. What can I do?"

Response: "What kind of medication is it?"

What rules are broken? ____

What categories does the responder place himself in? _________

____

What is the feeling being missed (expressed)? ________________

____

Write in your response ____

____

____

____

10.   A boy says to his father after a baseball game, "I got three hits and drove in the winning run!"

Response: "Hey, that's great! Did you have any errors this time?"

What rules are broken? _________________________________

What categories does the responder place himself in? _______

____

What is the feeling being missed (expressed)? ____________

____

Write in your response _______________________________

____

____

____

11.   A client says to an insurance agent, "I know I need medical insurance, but I'm so busy I can't seem to decide between two companies. I'll try to decide, but I have to be in Detroit tonight, a speech in New York tomorrow, a wedding sneaking up on me, and I have to attend my son's graduation Friday."

Response: "When can we talk about this again?"

What rules are broken? _________________________________

What categories does the responder place himself in? _______

____

What is the feeling being missed (expressed)? ____________

____

Write in your response _______________________________

____

____

12.   A father says to the family doctor, "My daughter's leg is broken in two places. The nurse who was there when she got hurt said we should possibly see a specialist. I'm afraid it is a bad injury and we hate to see her in so much pain. What do you think?"

Response: "Well you know this is not the first one of these I have done."

What rules are broken? ____

What categories does the responder place himself in? ________

____

What is the feeling being missed (expressed)? ________________

____

Write in your response ____

____

____

____

13.   A woman, divorced for two years, says to a priest, "As you know my husband was an alcoholic and was very sick. He abused the children. I didn't have any choice but to leave him. I don't like living alone and am thinking of getting married again. What do you think?"

Response: "Is your husband still living?"

What rules are broken? ____

What categories does the responder place himself in? ________

____

What is the feeling being missed (expressed)? ________________

____

Write in your response ____

____

____

14.   An outstanding high school football player says to the coach who is recruiting him, "It will be either Wisconsin or Northwestern. My Dad lives here in Madison and I would like to stay with my friends. My Mom lives just north of Evanston. Both my Mom and Dad want me to go to school close to them. I don't want to make either of them unhappy, I don't know what to do."

Response: "That makes it tough. What do you plan to major in, that could make a difference?"

What rules are broken? _______________________________

What categories does the responder place himself in? ________

____

What is the feeling being missed (expressed)? _______________

____

Write in your response _______________________________

____

____

____

I hope the examples provided here help readers to understand the book and recognize any "ingrainedness" or "LLPs" they might have lingering around. Many interactions, such as those just presented, occur everyday in our society. We *can* improve on our effectiveness when they arise. At the very least, it should be clear to all of us that "idle chatter" is no substitute for "communicating at a feeling level."

References

BENJAMIN, ALFRED. *The Helping Interview.* Boston: Houghton-Mifflin Co., 1969.

CARKHUFF, ROBERT R. and BERENSON, BERNARD G. *Beyond Counseling and Therapy.* New York: Holt, Rinehart and Winston, Inc., 1967.

EGAN, G. *The Skilled Helper.* Monterey, California: Brooks/Cole Publishing Company, 1975.

Interpersonal communication and the unseen power it holds in shaping us as individuals can be "lost in the shuffle" of our everyday activities. Perhaps the suggestions described in this book can increase our human potential to live harmoniously with one another.

It seems essential that if we choose to believe the concepts and ideas we became familiar with in this book, we not lose sight of the importance of interpersonal communication skills or allow them to "get lost in the shuffle." How important? We have already been familiarized with the devastating effects that poor communication can have on families, schools, and businesses, but we have not examined why this concept seems to be much more important today than it was twenty or thirty years ago. I am usually asked in teaching sessions why this seems to be true. My explanation is as follows.

The authoritarian approach to leadership and "people developing" *did,* in fact, work somewhat better many years ago because few people were aware of a better method. You may recall that the Hawthorne report demonstrated that a more democratic approach would not "sap the strength" of employees and could promote an atmosphere that assisted employees to "sense that someone was paying attention to them." Since that time the modernization of news reporting on Telstar, cable television, radio, telephone, the newspapers, and magazines, as well as other methods of receiving news quickly, has made the democratic process more familiar, more appealing, and acceptable to more people and at an earlier age. Our educational institutions emphasize the democratic process in many classes and our court system protects the rights of individuals to the point of disgust for those not informed of the laws concerning individual rights. All this "publicity" about the freedom that democracy brings with it has slowly taught more and more people that they should be treated in a humane, fair, and equal way. This knowledge and a natural inclination to be free, independent, and to have considerable say in their destiny has caused individuals and groups to lash back at any system that does not follow democratic principles. Minority groups, still suppressed, have fought for freedom, dignity, and "equal rights." Women's efforts for equal rights are an outgrowth of this knowledge supported by their feelings and thoughts of being treated in an inferior way. Students sitting down in front of, or actually taking over, university administration buildings were just another indication that authoritarian systems were being challenged, that the "publicity about democracy" was indeed "selling the product" rather well.

Research has for several years now strongly implied that authoritarian systems of organization and development fail, and fail miserably. As this "publicity" about the democratic way continues, the authoritarian approach will continue to die a slow death. This is the reason the human relations attitude described in these pages will be needed because the authoritarian approach is an *attitude* that must be replaced with a more democratic attitude. Our spoken words and the way we phrase them transmit one attitude or the other. The skills discussed here can assist us in accomplishing the task of delivering the words in such a way that the ineffective authoritarian method will no longer be needed.

My fear is that many readers, even though they are convinced the authoritarian system of communication and leadership should be eliminated, will cast aside the material as being gimmicky, insincere, corny, or, as has been written "a special language, blantantly artificial" (Gross, 1978). Do we really need conclusive scientific research studies to prove to us that there are many things in our personal communication that could be vastly improved?

As I stated at the beginning of this book, our LLPs run deep, very deep. It is difficult to understand how we willingly learn a complete foreign language, a sophisticated computer language, or even "footballese" so we can better understand Monday night football on television, but when it comes to the very well-being of our families, schools, and businesses, we term these new researched-based techniques as "gimmicky" or a "special language" instead of viewing them as an opportunity to develop a more democratic, humanistic attitude. I maintain that our LLPs are really the "special, artificial language" of which we should try and rid ourselves. Our customary way of communicating (LLPs) is the specially nutured language that causes so many of the problems in our society.

Another concern I have is that the concept we have just read about will be slightly misunderstood. A few people who have heard the ideas expressed here for the first time maintain that the concept conveys the permissive atmosphere where everyone from teenagers to employees "do their thing." The reason for this type attitude occurring is that we only know two systems of communication and of course they are autocratic and permissive. When we read or hear of response patterns that seemingly take our power away, we naturally think the atmosphere must be "powerless" which connotates permissiveness. Parents have often said to me, "We can't control our son or daughter anymore." More than likely the reason they can't "control" their off-spring anymore is that they tried to "control" them in the first place. This book was written with the intention of presenting to people the ideas and concepts that help us to give up the dangerous power game in our personal communication and feel good about it while being effective in working with others or at least feel as though we have things under control.

Of course, in order to do this we must perceive ourselves some-what differently. We must learn to look at our actions, our LLPs, body LLPs, and develop courage to change those traits we now see need to be changed.

My theory on what must happen to bring about this desirable change is not, to be sure, a universally accepted theory. However, it does seem to me that we must feel somewhat uneasy, doubtful, possibly guilty, and extremely challenged in order to make changes in something that has been with us for a long time. The needed change won't come easily! If it doesn't come easily then it will no doubt create some "uncomfortableness" within us. I think the process we are looking for must "tug at our gut" a little bit. If it isn't "tugging" it probably isn't taking effect. To really look at how we "come across to people" with our form of communication is not usually voluntarily undertaken. The fact is, it *is* uncomfortable at first when we attempt to make a change. The implementation process creates a feeling in many people that they aren't being sincere and most of us don't enjoy a feeling of insincerity. In spite of this, we still have to consider all of the obstacles to good communication and weigh the harm we frequently transmit. We can compare this ineffectiveness to a short period of learning time and of being uncomfortable and thinking we aren't being sincere. *Thinking* we are sincere and *being* sincere, as we have learned, are often two different things. It also seems true that young people learn to determine whether or not a person *is* being sincere. Since most adults want to be sincere when working with young people, it becomes confusing and very difficult for adults to make these changes.

Often times it seems that people have to become down and

out or really discouraged before they can accept the idea that communication can have a tremendous affect on their lives. Allow me to offer one final thought about this!

Can our LLPs cause mental illness? *If* we count admissions to mental health facilities as a way of tracing or counting incidences of mental illness in our society, then I think the answer is a resounding yes. In the past several years I have seen scores of young people admitted to these facilities. These young people are taken out of their normal environment, thoroughly tested, evaluated physically and mentally, and, after a period of "being away from those who reported them to be ill" they often "improved." Amazing! Various reasons are given for this "improvement." No real proof exists, of course, possibly because we aren't looking for any; but our LLPs, verbal muggings, discouraging words, power type communication, and "feelingless responses" may be *partially* to blame for the creation of these unfortunate occurrences.

It may be possible, with ineffective communication, to literally "drive someone crazy," especially our vulnerable young people. Young people are not allowed "to do the driving." Adults make all of the decisions about admissions to mental health facilities. Since we might agree now that a vast majority of adults are not aware of the devastating effects of our LLPs, they cannot recognize when the LLPs might be the real reason admission to a mental health facility is "recommended." Adults *do* know, however, when they become discouraged as a result of the LLPs used by their youngsters to fight back. Remember Danny? When the adults have "had enough" or become so scared or very discouraged they have the youngster "admitted." I have never heard of a youngster being allowed to have his or her parents or "significant" adult admitted to a mental health facility. This phenomenon of youngsters being admitted for mental health care is, to my way of thinking, one of the most subtle types of child abuse we have going in our society. To be sure, I am not saying that the mental health experts can't help, they often can, but it is just the idea of whose LLPs they are concentrating on! The mental health facilities need to be there, if for no other reason than that the LLPs used there are a little less devastating than they are elsewhere in our society.

How important is it to understand the overall effects of our LLPs? Actually that is an individual choice. It has been my goal to provide some data so you, a parent, teacher, nurse, counselor, psychologist, executive, manager, lawyer, or salesperson can make an informed choice. If we can agree that interpersonal communication can have effect on our lives in such important matters as the learning process, marriage, business, and our schools and families it seems we might also agree that progression through a life of devastating LLPs could possibly cause mental illness. With this in mind we might be able to motivate ourselves to implement programs to prevent some of the costly results brought about by our LLPs. The skills will not be implemented by chance. We must design programs to *specifically* help people develop these skills.

My suggestion to implement these skills into our society doesn't involve learning new words or a different language. It really means rearranging words we already know. It means rearranging our attitudes. It does take time and study along with some motivation and desire. Learning not to bat crosshanded as a youngster learning to play baseball also took some motivation. As stated earlier, the implementation process may be uncomfortable and will feel "gimmicky" as we go through it. Diabetics have to learn how to take insulin and that is quite a change when they haven't experienced it before. Few will tell us it is comfortable initially, but most will tell us it was a life or death decision. Our personal communications are nearly as important.

Quality, as well as quantity, in life is something to consider, and our interpersonal communication style can add to or subtract from that quality. Good communication is the insulin, the lifeline of human relationships.

So much is ingrained within us that we could never remove all of the obstacles in the way of good communication, but if we can eliminate some of them, at least in some situations, we can develop better harmony among us. We can do it! As someone once said, "Life is an endless process of self-discovery."

Reference

GROSS, MARTIN. *The Psychological Society.* New York: Random House, Inc., 1978.

Bibliography

ANTHONY, WILLIAM and CARKHUFF, ROBERT R. *The Art of Health Care.* Amherst, Mass.: Human Resource Developmental Press, Inc., 1976.

BANVILLE, THOMAS G. *How to Listen—How to Be Heard.* Chicago: Nelson-Hall, 1978.

BENJAMIN, ALFRED. *The Helping Interview.* Boston: Houghton-Mifflin Co., 1969.

CARKHUFF, ROBERT R. and BERENSON, BERNARD G. *Beyond Counseling and Therapy.* New York: Holt, Rinehart and Winston, Inc., 1967.

DINKMEYER, DON and McKAY, GARY D. *Systematic Training for Effective Parenting: Parents Handbook,* Circle Pines, Minnesota: American Guidance Service, Inc., 1976.

DREIKURS, RUDOLF and CASSEL, PEARL. *Discipline Without Tears.* New York: Hawthorn Books, Inc., 1972. (Now Hawthorn/Dutton)

EGAN, G. *The Skilled Helper.* Monterey, California: Brooks/Cole Publishing Co., 1975.

GALLUP, GEORGE. Tenth Annual Gallup Poll of the Public's Attitude Toward Public Schools. *American Educator,* Winter, 1978, p. 5.

GAZDA, G. M. *et al. Human Relations Development: A Manual for Educators.* Boston: Copyright © 1973 by Allyn and Bacon, Inc.

GORDON, THOMAS. *Parent Effectiveness Training.* © 1970. Reprinted with permission from the book *Parent Effectiveness Training* by Gordon. Copyright © 1970. Published by David McKay Co., Inc.

GORDON, THOMAS. *L.E.T. Leader Effectiveness Training.* Reprinted with permission of Wyden Books from *L.E.T. Leader Effectiveness Training* by Dr. Thomas Gordon. Copyright © 1977 by Dr. Thomas Gordon.

GROSS, MARTIN. *The Psychological Society.* New York: Random House, Inc., 1978.

LAIR, JESS. *"I Ain't Much Baby—But I'm All I've Got."* New York: Fawcett Publications, Inc. 1969, 1972. (Doubleday and Company)

LILLIBRIDGE, MICHAEL E. and KLUKKEN, GARY. Interpersonal Communication Skills, Cassette Tape Series, Affective House, Tulsa, Oklahoma, 1977.

LOSONCY, LEWIS. *Turning People On: How to Be an Encouraging Person.* © 1977. Reprinted by permission of Prentice-Hall, Inc., Englewood Cliffs, New Jersey.

MOUSTAKES, C. *Who Will Listen?.* New York: Ballantine Books (A Division of Random House), 1975.

POWELL, JOHN S. J. *Why Am I Afraid to Tell You Who I Am?.* Niles, Illinois: Argus Communications. © 1969.

SHERTZER, B. and STONE, S. *Fundamentals of Guidance.* Boston: Houghton-Mifflin Co., 1976.

SUGARMAN, DANIEL A. *Priceless Gifts.* Copyright © 1978. New York: Macmillian Publishing Company, 1978.

TIME, The Weekly Magazine. Reprinted by permission from TIME, The Weekly Magazine; Copyright © Time, Inc., 1978. (Excerpt from article "Middletown Revisited," October, 1976.)

Other Suggested Readings

DINKMEYER, DON and LOSONCY, LEWIS. *The Encouragement Book.* Englewood Cliffs, New Jersey: Prentice-Hall, Inc., 1980.

DINKMEYER, DON and DREIKURS, RUDOLF. *Encouraging Children to Learn: The Encouragement Process.* Englewood Cliffs, New Jersey: Prentice-Hall, 1963. New York: Elsevier-Dutton, 1979.

LONG, LYNETTE. *Listening/Responding: Human Relations Training for Teachers.* Monterey, California: Brooks/Cole Publishing Company, 1978.

LOSONCY, LEWIS E. *You Can Do It: How to Encourage Yourself.* Englewood Cliffs, New Jersey: Prentice-Hall, 1980.

Index